www.amelia-king.com
Get in touch! hello@amelia-king.com

Thinking with AI

Amelia King

Thinking
EdTech

THINKING WITH AI

Contents

For J, the best thinker I know.

A quick note before we begin...

As everything in this book talks about ethical and thoughtful use of AI, I figured it was just as important to be transparent about how I use AI to develop my own content.

Throughout the journey of writing Thinking with AI, I used a range of AI tools (both generative and non-generative) to support the process. Specifically:

- **Fireflies AI** (or similar transcription tools) used to transcribe voice notes and conversations with others, helping me capture my ideas quickly and accurately.
- **Claude 3.5 and 3.7** by Anthropic helped me improve the flow and clarity of those often jumbled first voice notes.
- **Perplexity** and **Consensus** were used, alongside traditional non-AI tools, to find research papers both new and old.
- **Google NotebookLM** was used as a research hub where I could hold the research papers I held and interrogate them; though I checked all usage in my own work, any further citation errors are human fault rather than AI!

Importantly, nothing in this book was published as-is from AI tools. Every element has been carefully reviewed, edited, and developed by me. I use AI as a tool to support my own creativity, thought process, and overall clarity, but never as a replacement for expertise, quality, or integrity.

In other words, the thinking is all me... for better, or for worse.

Introduction

Imagine an office building. Now, imagine one so enormous that you can't see the end of it. Imagine, if you will, a Stupidly Large Office Building (SLOB). And now, as delicately as possible, please place 86 billion workers inside it.

Ready?

Then let's begin.

Each worker in this building has a very simple job: they can either shout "YES!" or stay quiet. That's it. They can't speak in sentences, they can't write essays, they can't do maths—all they can do is either make noise or not make noise.

Now, these workers are incredibly social. Each one is connected to thousands of other workers through a sort of internal telephone system. When Worker 74 shouts "YES!", all the other workers connected to Worker 74 hear it through their phones and they, too, will continue the shout. If Worker 878,451 then gets the "YES!" call, then they're pretty likely to also shout "YES!" and trigger all of their connected phones.

In essence, we end up with a sort of cascade effect—one worker shouts, which makes their connected workers more likely to shout, which makes their connected workers shout, and so on.

It gets a little more complicated than that, though. Specific patterns of workers shouting together actually represent different things. For example, when Workers 1, 47, 293, 1,847, and 23,891 all shout together, that pattern means *apple*. When Workers 15, 203, 1,203, and 9,847 shout together, that pattern means *bicycle*. These patterns have been created and learned by the workers over an extended period of time. The more often a particular group of workers shout together to form their given pattern, the stronger their phone connections become. It's like they install better phone lines between them, or turn up the volume, or add entirely new phone lines altogether.

When new information—such as new patterns, or even new concepts made of a bunch of different patterns—first arrives at SLOB, it stops at the reception desk in the lobby. The receptionist's job is to briefly hold this new information while deciding what to do with it. Should it be sent up to the workers? Is it important enough to disturb the office? Does it connect to any existing worker groups? And so on.

The only problem is that the receptionist has two very specific limitations: he can literally only handle about four pieces of incoming information at once before he becomes completely overwhelmed, and he can only hold onto a piece of information for about 15 to 30 seconds before it gets bumped out by newer information. If you want something to stick around longer, he needs to keep actively repeating it (like when you repeat a phone number to yourself), or find a way to connect it to the worker groups upstairs.

When the receptionist decides information is worth keeping, he starts sending messages up to relevant worker groups in the building, and that's when the "YES!" or *apple* patterns start to get sent out through the SLOB phone lines.

Every night when SLOB goes into 'maintenance mode', office management reviews the day's communication patterns. They look at which worker groups have been active, which phone connections have been used most, and which ones seem important enough to make permanent.

They then do two things:

1. Worker groups that fired together during the day get their phone connections further upgraded. The maintenance crew installs even better equipment, adds more phone lines, and sometimes

even relocates workers closer together for more efficient communication.

2. Just as importantly, phone lines that weren't used much get disconnected. Workers who haven't been communicating with each other lose their connections. This isn't wasteful, it's essential. The building has limited resources, and maintaining unused phone lines is inefficient.

The conversation goes something like this: "Workers 47 and 1,847 have been talking constantly about *apple*, so let's give them a direct hotline. But workers 203 and 9,847 haven't spoken about *bicycle* in months, so let's disconnect that line and use those resources elsewhere."

Still with me? Then please take a moment to appreciate the following fun fact: **Your brain contains 86 billion specialised cells called 'neurons'.**

"Wait a minute," I hear you say, "isn't that the same number of workers currently employed at the Stupidly Large Office Building?"

Let me explain...

You see, each of the 86 billion neurons in your brain has a very simple function: it can either fire an electrical impulse or remain inactive; that is to say, it can shout, "YES!" or stay silent. Much like the SLOB workers, individual neurons can't store complex thoughts, create essays, or solve mathematical problems. They can either shout, or not shout. That's it.

And, just like the workers at SLOB, these 86 billion neurons are incredibly interconnected. Each one connects to thousands of others through tiny gaps called synapses. These tiny gaps are incredibly small—and by 'incredibly small', we're talking fitting-2000-ish-synapses-across-the-width-of-a-single-human-hair kind of incredibly small. When a neuron fires an electrical impulse, it releases chemical messengers called neurotransmitters into these synaptic gaps. These are the phone calls our office workers are making whenever management (i.e., You) request a new concept.

Connected neurons receive these chemical phone calls through special receptor proteins on their surface. If enough neurotransmitters reach the receiving neuron simultaneously, then that receiving neuron will also fire an electrical impulse and release its own neurotransmitters to its connected neurons. Neuron after neuron, worker after worker, phone call after phone call, creating cascade effects throughout your brain. Specific combinations of neurons firing together represent different pieces of information; one group might represent the concept of *apple*, whilst another could be *bicycle*, with specific neural patterns being developed through repeated experience.

The more often particular groups of neurons fire together, the stronger their synaptic connections become. So if you think about *apples* frequently, the synaptic connections between the neurons in your *apple* network become increasingly strong and reliable. Eventually, activating just part of this network can trigger the entire pattern—perhaps just seeing the colour red is enough to cascade through strengthened synapses and activate your complete understanding of *apples*. Conversely, if you very rarely think about obscure information like *the capital of Mongolia*, those synaptic connections remain weak. The neurons reduce neurotransmitter production, receptor proteins are removed from cell membranes, and the physical structure of the synapses actually shrinks. Eventually, your brain prunes away these unused connections to conserve metabolic resources. This is the biological basis of forgetting—or, in other words, management cuts the phone line.

So, I hear you ask, what does this have to do with Artificial Intelligence in education?

Well, it turns out, a heck of a lot.

Before we get into the book proper, let's take one more look at two different versions of the Stupidly Large Office Building. The first SLOB belongs to a student named Janine. The second, to one called Kiki.

Recently, Janine's receptionist has discovered that there's this incredible external service called AI Corp that can handle almost any request she sends them. Need an essay written? AI Corp delivers it instantly. Want a maths problem solved? Done. Need to analyse a text? No problem. Janine's receptionist quickly learns that they don't really need to process incoming information anymore. When new information arrives—let's say a complex maths problem—instead of trying to understand it and send messages to the relevant worker groups upstairs, the receptionist just forwards it straight to AI Corp.

The receptionist thinks, "Why bother figuring out what this means or which workers need to handle it? AI Corp will sort it out." So the receptionist stops doing the hard work of analysing, categorising, and making connections.

Remember our workers? The maths workers, the writing workers, the analysis workers—they all start getting fewer and fewer messages from the receptionist. When a maths problem comes in, instead of the receptionist sending it upstairs to the maths workers so they can fire together and strengthen their connections, the problem just gets outsourced. The maths workers sit around with nothing to do.

This is where we see our first problem. Remember how worker groups strengthen their connections by firing together—making those connected phone calls—repeatedly? Well, if they're not firing together because all the work is being sent elsewhere, their phone lines start to weaken. The maintenance crew looks around during the nightly maintenance and thinks, "These phone lines between the maths workers haven't been used in weeks. We need those resources elsewhere." So they start disconnecting the lines and reassigning the maintenance budget to other parts of the building.

Then, those rich networks that connect different worker groups? They start falling apart.

So let's say Janine needs to solve a word problem that involves both maths and reading comprehension. In a well-functioning office building, the reading workers would communicate with the maths workers, who would talk to the problem-solving workers, who would coordinate with the logic workers.

But Janine's workers have lost the ability to communicate effectively with each other. When the receptionist gets the word problem, they just send the whole thing to AI Corp without any internal processing.

Over time, something fundamental changes in Janine's office building. The workers stop developing problem-solving skills. They lose confidence in their ability to handle challenges independently. When faced with any complex task, the first instinct becomes send it to AI Corp rather than let's figure this out together. The building develops a learned helplessness—workers literally forget how to work together to solve problems.

When AI Corp sends back solutions, Janine's workers don't really engage with them. They don't think, "Oh, this connects to what we learnt about fractions last month," or "This reminds me of that chemistry concept."

The solutions just pass through the building. Connection-less.

And so, after months of this pattern, something alarming happens: Janine's office building becomes completely dependent on AI Corp. When AI Corp isn't available, the building simply can't function. The workers have lost their skills, their connections to each other have weakened, and they've forgotten how to tackle problems independently. The receptionist doesn't even know which worker groups to contact for different types of problems anymore.

Then there's Kiki.

Kiki's receptionist has discovered the same external service that Janine uses—AI Corp—but she approaches it completely differently. Kiki sees AI Corp not as a replacement for her office building's work, but as a powerful consultant that can support and enhance what her workers do.

When a complex problem arrives—say, a challenging essay assignment about climate change—Kiki's receptionist doesn't immediately forward it to AI Corp. Instead, the receptionist does something clever. First, they analyse the request: "Right, this is asking for an argumentative essay. That means we need our research workers, our writing workers, our critical thinking workers, and our organisation workers all involved. But before we start, let me see what we already know."

The receptionist sends messages upstairs: "Research team, what do we already know about climate change? Writing team, what do we remember about essay structure? Critical thinking team, what are the key questions we should be asking?"

Kiki's worker groups spring into action. They start firing together, making connections, pulling up what they already know. After this initial brainstorming—that is, after her workers have done some genuine thinking—Kiki decides to bring in AI Corp as a consultant.

Kiki's receptionist sends a carefully crafted message to AI Corp: "We're working on understanding the economic impacts of carbon pricing policies. We've identified three key areas we want to explore: impact on small businesses, effects on consumer behaviour, and international competitiveness. Can you help us find current research and data on these specific aspects?"

When AI Corp sends back detailed research, something crucial happens in Kiki's building: her workers don't just passively accept it. Instead, they actively engage with the information. The research workers examine the data and think, "How does this connect to what we learned about carbon markets last month?" The critical thinking workers ask,

"What are the limitations of these studies? What questions aren't being addressed?"

The receptionist coordinates this process: "Research team, integrate this new information with our existing knowledge. Critical thinking team, identify any gaps or contradictions. Writing team, start thinking about how to structure an argument that incorporates both our prior knowledge and this new research."

When the research workers connect the new carbon pricing data to their existing economics knowledge, those phone lines between worker groups get reinforced. The maintenance crew notices increased activity and strengthens these connections during nightly maintenance.

Over time, something wonderful happens: Kiki's office building becomes more capable than it would have been without AI Corp support, but also—and here's the really fun part—also more capable than *other* buildings that rely too heavily on AI Corp.

But how is this possible?

Because Kiki uses AI Corp to tackle more challenging problems than she could handle alone, while still doing the cognitive work necessary to learn and grow.

She might use AI Corp to access cutting-edge research that would take her hours to find independently, then spend her cognitive energy on the higher-level work of synthesis, analysis, and original thinking. She's amplifying her capabilities rather than replacing them.

The fundamental difference between Kiki and Janine isn't the company they keep (or the technology they use)—it's how they use it. Janine uses AI Corp to avoid cognitive work; Kiki uses AI Corp to enhance cognitive work. Janine's building atrophies because it stops being challenged; Kiki's building grows stronger because it's appropriately challenged with good support.

This is the difference between AI Corp as a cognitive crutch versus AI Corp as a cognitive amplifier. The same tool, used in completely different ways, with completely different outcomes for learning and development.

And that's what this book is about. How do we ensure we have cohorts of students who are Kikis, rather than Janines?

Read on to find out.

Critical Thinking

1

What exactly is critical thinking?

For the majority of the first term of high school, my entire year group was timetabled for a weekly Critical Thinking lesson led by the scariest (and therefore, best) teacher in the English department. The lessons were intended to help us become better thinkers, better consumers of the world around us, and ultimately better students.

Unfortunately, the only thing I remember from those lessons is the time I had to colour in a picture of a human brain to show the 'different areas that thinking took place'. There were a few study skills sessions thrown in, but for a kid who was far more comfortable writing out my notes a dozen times until I had rote-learned them than actually using any genuine study techniques, none of it really stuck. So for the longest time, critical thinking to me was some ephemeral task nestled somewhere between 'extra work for no reward' and 'just thinking, but fancy.'

I was almost right.

Critical thinking isn't just another type of thinking. It's not just 'thinking, but fancy.' There are steps to thinking critically. There are, would you believe, definitions.

Critical thinking requires you to analyse, evaluate, and synthesise information. You need to be reflective and to criticise your underlying assumptions. There are a number of different cognitive processes at play that allow you to come to a reasoned conclusion. There's even the classic Bloom's Taxonomy with its concepts like analyse and evaluate that can help you distinguish between lower-order thinking and the more critical levels. (Don't worry, we'll get to Bloom's in more detail soon enough!

In other words, critical thinking is thinking deeply, not just thinking.

One way to determine whether you're thinking critically or just thinking comes from Daniel Willingham, Professor of Psychology at the University of Virginia. He argues that critical thinking needs three things:

- **Novelty**: Not just recalling information or applying knowledge, but coming up with new thoughts and ideas.
- **Self-direction**: Coming up with your own ideas, not just following instructions or the guidance of others.
- **Effectiveness**: Your thinking needs to achieve something, which means you need to be thinking with a specific goal in mind.

This checklist is a great tool to keep in mind as we move through the next few chapters. At all times, you can use it to consider whether an activity enables critical thinking or not. Let's take a look at it in context to really understand how it could work.

* * *

Imagine a history classroom where students are studying the Treaty of Versailles, the agreement signed after the end of World War I that, arguably, was one of the major causes of the rise of Nazi Germany and eventually World War II.

A surface-level thinking task might ask students to list the key terms of the Treaty so that they can later refer back to these for an essay or other synthesis activity. The task is simple enough that a student might just Google *list of terms treaty of versailles*, copy the list, and consider the task complete. Or perhaps, considering the age we now live in, they could request the same from an AI tool knowing that it might give them slightly more 'human' phrasing.

But looking through the lens of Willingham's definition, we can see immediately that there's no critical thinking taking place. There's no novelty; they're just retrieving existing facts. There's little self-direction, because they're following the task to the letter without making choices. Effectiveness is minimal: the student can repeat information but hasn't done anything with it.

Don't get me wrong, there's nothing wrong with a task like this; you need basic knowledge in order to think critically moving forward. There is always a place for this surface-level thinking in the classroom. But the thinking is not *critical.*

Let's take the exercise a little further, just to really cement our understanding of what critical thinking really is. Instead of asking students to list terms, perhaps you ask "Which term of the Treaty of Versailles do you think had the most significant impact on Germany in the 1920s? Justify your answer with evidence and consider an alternative viewpoint."

Now we're cooking:

- **Novelty**: The student isn't just repeating facts. They must decide which term was most significant, which means they're coming up with something new. Note that novelty doesn't necessarily mean 'entirely new idea that no one in the history of humanity has ever considered.' It's okay if novelty is just something new to the thinker.
- **Self-direction**: The student chooses their own evidence and argument, rather than simply copying ideas, or following instructions to come to a regimented output.
- **Effectiveness**: The student must justify their point (accomplishing the thinking goal) and should do this with relevant evidence and multiple perspectives.

This is a great example of critical thinking in action.

But this is a book about AI and thinking, not just students and thinking. Right? Well, let's give the same critical question to Chat GPT and see what it has to say:

> *By draining state finances, triggering hyper-inflation, and shaping international diplomacy, reparations became the pivot around which Germany's economic, social, and political crises revolved.*
>
> *Mechanisms of Impact and Evidence:*

- *Fiscal drain and inflationary financial impact: • By 1923 Germany had paid only 4.2 billion gold marks in cash and kind, yet the government's attempt to keep up payments by printing marks fuelled the hyper-inflation of 1922-23 (a loaf of bread: 250 marks in Jan 1923 → 200 billion in Nov 1923)• Middle-class savings were wiped out*
- *Direct foreign coercion: • When Germany fell behind on deliveries, French and Belgian troops occupied the Ruhr (Jan 1923), seizing its industrial heartland.• Passive resistance, financed by the Reich, cost roughly twice the annual reparations bill, deepening the fiscal crisis and unemployment.*
- *International leverage over German sovereignty: • The Dawes Plan (1924) and Young Plan (1929) re-scheduled payments but at the price of foreign supervision of the Reichsbank and railways.• Reparations became the bargaining chip for Germany's gradual diplomatic rehabilitation (Locarno, League of Nations entry) but also a constant reminder of dependence.*
- *Political polarisation:• Right-wing parties and the nascent Nazi movement used reparations and the "tribute" narrative to brand Weimar politicians as "November criminals."• The 1929 referendum on the Young Plan, though defeated, mobilised 5.8 million "anti-tribute" votes, showing the clause's enduring emotional power.*

Some historians argue that the war-guilt clause had the deepest psychological effect because it:

- *Provided the legal basis for reparations, thereby humiliating Germans twice—morally and materially.*
- *Fueled nationalist resentment and the "stab-in-the-back" myth, eroding legitimacy of democratic leaders.*

Counter-argument

- *While Article 231 undoubtedly wounded national pride, its material consequences were indirect; without the accompanying reparations schedule its practical impact would have been limited*
- *Political mobilisation against Versailles in the 1920s almost always returned to concrete hardships—bankruptcies, unemployment, and tax burdens—stemming from reparations rather than from abstract guilt*
- *The fact that agitation subsided temporarily during the "Golden Years" (1924-28) when payments were softened shows that economic relief muted the psychological grievance*

Conclusion

All Versailles terms damaged the fledgling Weimar state, but reparations translated humiliation into daily economic pain, provoked foreign intervention, and gave extremists a tangible rallying cry. Their cascading effects—from hyper-inflation to the Ruhr crisis and perpetual fiscal instability—made the reparations clause the single most consequential element of the treaty for Germany in the 1920s.

Now, as a history teacher, I'm pretty happy with this response. It's a good, if basic, outline of what could eventually become a clear argumentative essay. My AI student has given me not only a list of key reasons why it thinks reparations were the most consequential clause of the Treaty of Versailles, but it backs up the reasons with numerous clear examples. There's a good counter-argument (although it could be more detailed), and the beginnings of a good conclusion. And honestly, if a student submitted this to me, then a surface level glance could tell me that this response definitely fits Willingham's three requirements for critical thinking. My 'student' has given me their own reasons for their argument, which arguably could be considered novelty. They've directed themselves by selecting and backing up which point they think is strongest. And their thinking is effective because they were able to come to a reasoned conclusion about which term was the most damaging.

So there we have it, folks. The illusion of critical thinking, completed simply by copying the teacher's question into an AI tool and sharing the answer.

Welcome to the AI world.

Even before the proliferation of generative AI tools in the classroom, students were finding ways to offload their thinking to other sources of information. Whether it was copying information from a library book, grabbing research from Wikipedia, or simply copying your homework from a classmate. This is nothing new. What is new is the ease at which students today can offload not just their thinking, but their critical thinking as well, as seen in the answer above. Worse, they can adjust the AI output to make it even more difficult for teachers to track what thinking has actually taken place. Students can ask AI to write its response like an 11-year-old, or in the student's own voice, or for a particular reading level. There have even been cases where college students have asked an AI tool to keep certain mistakes in its response to make it more believable.

(The question of whether this type of prompting could actually be a form of critical thinking is up for debate).

Here's something else to consider: studies show that children in particular are more likely to trust a robot—or in our case, an AI tool—if they like it. Now, if we argue that AI tools are trained to be agreeable with the user (and indeed, they can border on sycophantic when the training goes wrong), then it's likely that the children and young people using the AI tool will 'like' the AI that they are speaking to. Pull that knowledge together along with research that shows knowledge workers use less critical thinking the more they trust what the output is telling them, and suddenly you have a perfect storm for a reduction in critical thinking in our students.

Worse, critical thinking is a cognitive skill that, just like a muscle, gets weaker over time if it's not being used enough. A 2025 study found exactly this; overreliance on AI is clearly linked to reduced critical thinking and acceptance of basic answers that just 'get the job done'. That means that not only are students potentially not engaging in critical thinking, but it might just be that no one realises this is happening, and thus the critical thinking skills of our students may diminish over time before we notice.

So what do we do about it?

Unfortunately, the cat is out of the bag, and there's no way to get it back in.

Various studies from around the world are telling us that anywhere from 65% to 74% or more of school-aged students have at least dabbled with generative AI. With so many other factors impacting how students engage with their learning, one thing we can be certain about is that this proportion is not likely to decrease any time soon.

If we're not getting rid of it, then, we've got to work with it. In other words, we need to explicitly teach pupils to think alongside AI in order to prevent them from getting AI to do their thinking for them. Luckily for us as educators, AI is secretly nothing special.

I know, I was shocked too.

But here's the secret... we can treat AI like nearly every other information source we use in the classroom today: by questioning, comparing, and using it with intention.

In his book *Co-Intelligence*, Ethan Mollick offers a helpful distinction between two different ways we might use generative AI. In Mollick's view, what we're looking at is working as either a centaur or a cyborg:

- **Centaur**: Human and AI thinking are distinct. The human does the thinking first, then uses AI as a tool. You can see the difference between the two, and someone using AI can share roughly which elements of a task was completed by an AI tool versus by the human.
- **Cyborg**: Human and AI thinking are fused, with a back-and-forth partnership. You can't really tell the difference between the two, and you can't see where one ends and one begins.

Both approaches have a place in the classroom. After all, sometimes you want students to do the thinking first and then use AI to check or expand on their ideas. Other times, you want them to use AI as a partner, going back and forth and building on each other's contributions. In other words, sometimes you want students to Think, With AI (that is, do their human thinking and then their AI thinking, working as a centaur), and sometimes you want them to Think with AI (working as a cyborg). Again, what we're looking at here is being intentional with AI use. In the words of a previous colleague of mine, Kelly King, we're looking at using AI by design, not just by default.

What matters here is that you're not leaving AI use to chance. You're building in specific opportunities to use AI in the classroom so that you can develop students' skills to thinking critically before, during, and after AI use. If you don't intentionally build in opportunities for students to critique AI, it won't happen. AI offers the illusion of authority, and students aren't content experts—they won't naturally critique what it gives them, and often won't know how to do so even if they want to. Various studies have shown that content experts benefit the most from AI as they know the right questions to ask. If AI is going to become the norm, both in education or in the wider workforce, then we need to prepare our students for this new way of thinking.

So I'm going to split this section into two parts. First, we'll look at how we can encourage students to think critically about AI <u>input</u>. Then, we'll do the same with AI <u>output</u>. Remember to take each of these with a grain of salt; not every task is going to suit every classroom, nor is every question relevant for the age or subject you teach.

Take what works, bin the rest.

Just like using AI, really.

2

Thinking critically about AI input

If you want critical thinking to be at the forefront of a student's mind when they use AI, then critical thinking needs to be encouraged from the very first stages of AI use. In fact, it should go back even earlier than that; students need to use critical thinking to decide how, and even if, they're going to use AI in the first place.

One of the simplest ways to explain why this matters is the old computing principle of "garbage in, garbage out." If the instructions going into the AI are unclear, shallow, or confused, the output will be too. It's not that the AI is wrong—it's simply doing what you told it to do! A prompt like *Tell me about Shakespeare* will inevitably give you a bland, general answer because the AI has no sense of what you actually care about or what you're actually wanting to find out. But a more thoughtful prompt—maybe something like *Summarise the plot of Macbeth in under 200 words for someone who's never read it, focusing on the theme of ambition*—is far more likely to produce something relevant, concise, and useful. Really, the work here isn't actually about what the AI prompt ends up being, it's in the thinking before the typing: *Who is this for? What do I actually need? How detailed should it be?* That reflection is where the critical thinking begins.

It's important to be aware that good prompting is also very rarely a one-shot deal. It's a process with the best results coming from iteration, where you are refining and improving what you're asking as you go. This is where students can treat AI as a partner in thinking rather than a vending machine for answers. The first prompt might be broad, just to get a feel for what's possible. The second builds on that: narrowing focus, adding context, or asking for a specific lens. The third tests the limits: changing format, shifting audience, or adding a comparison. Each turn is a chance to spot gaps, clarify intent, and push for deeper insight. In doing so, students are practising exactly the skills we want in critical thinking—identifying what's missing, questioning assumptions, and deliberately moving closer to a goal rather than settling for whatever appears first on the screen.

But there's a not-so-hidden risk in prompting too precisely. If students over-specify what they want—*Give me exactly five bullet points, each eight words long, using only past tense, including a relevant quote*—they may get exactly what they asked for, but not necessarily what they actually needed. Worse, depending on the AI tool they're using, technical limitations or AI hallucinations (where the AI tool could make up a plausible-sounding quote or reference) might mean they don't even get what they want in the first place! Overly rigid prompts can strip away opportunities for unexpected insights or richer perspectives. If every prompt is built to confirm what the student already thinks, they'll never be surprised. And surprise, in learning, is often the spark that leads to curiosity and deeper exploration. The balance is to keep prompts clear enough to guide the AI, but open enough to allow it to introduce something the student hadn't considered.

Recent studies show that iterating on an initial prompt can help a knowledge worker develop critical thinking by forcing them to narrow in on what they really want from the AI. Working to improve AI input is therefore an ideal way to begin the critical thinking process. One useful way to frame this is through the three principles we looked at earlier with Professor Willingham: novelty, self-direction, and effectiveness.

Novelty

Remember that novelty is about creating something new, not just rote repetition of already known facts. Getting into the habit of asking AI to complete every task for you is not novel, even if you ostensibly end up with a novel output. With that in mind, if there's a chance of students using AI for a task, get them to ask themselves: *Is this task something where using AI will help me produce something new, or am I just repeating a pattern (e.g., always using AI without thought)?* Note how this puts the power in the students' hands; they're the ones who are working out whether the task is worth using AI for or not. This line of questioning could also result in the student deciding not to use AI at all, or perhaps to brainstorm ideas on their own first, then check with AI for gaps or alternative perspectives, moving between a centaur or cyborg relationship depending on the needs of the task.

With that in mind, why not try the following ideas to find a balance between AI-free and AI-augmented novelty:

- **First-draft challenge:** Students must produce their own answer or plan before touching AI, then compare the two and annotate what's truly new in the AI's suggestions.

- **Reverse prompting:** Give students an AI answer and have them write the prompt they think generated it. Discuss how vague prompts lead to generic answers.
- **Novelty filter:** After AI produces something, students highlight what is unique vs. what they could have produced without it.

Self-direction

One way of ensuring self-direction in AI use is by giving the student the chance to make the decision themselves about how and if they might use AI for a task, rather than getting them to follow teacher-provided instructions (such as the increasingly common AI usage scales that range from "no AI usage" to "AI is magical let's go wild"). This one can be more difficult to fully support as it depends on a number of factors, including both the age of the student and their skills/confidence with AI. Sometimes, a teacher might need to be more didactic in their instructions on how and if to use AI. That might remove the self-direction element and perhaps turn the task into more of a guided activity. But that's okay! Sometimes you can find critical thinking in other areas of the task.

If we're talking full independence and self-direction, however, then encourage the student to again question their AI use: *Do I need clarification? Do I want AI to check my logic? Would using AI here shortcut my own thinking?* In an ideal world (read: in a world with well-trained and highly motivated students!), the student might reflect on their AI use by going, "I'm struggling to generate arguments for this topic; maybe I'll ask AI for counterpoints, but I'll write my own main argument." They're already thinking critically before they begin to use the AI tool!

Some more activities that might work in your classroom could include:

- **Decision journal:** Students keep a short log of when they use AI, why they chose to, and what other options they considered. You may even wish to include a self-reflection element as part of your assessment rubric.
- **AI pause button:** Before typing a prompt, students answer three quick questions: "Do I need clarification? Do I want AI to check my thinking? Would using AI shortcut my own learning?"
- **Role-swap debate:** Half the class argues for using AI on a given task, the other against. Swap halfway and see if opinions shift. Use this to help your class determine whether the activity is an appropriate time to use AI. You could even keep a record of opinions to reuse in future AI/no AI debates.

Effectiveness

This is often the trickiest part of the three to fully grasp. After all, how can I determine if my thinking is effective? That's why sometimes it's easier to think in terms of whether your thinking has an ultimate purpose, relevance, or outcome. Each of these can show that thinking is effective.

You could also consider effectiveness through the lens of Bloom's Taxonomy; whether the thinking involves applying, analysing, evaluating or creating (more on this in Chapter 5!). Ultimately, the student's decision on whether to use AI or not should revolve around whether it will be purposeful use, rather than just getting things done faster or easier In this case they might ask things like: *Will using AI here actually help me learn, or will it undermine my skills? Is there a smarter way to use AI—say, for feedback rather than for content generation?*

This train of thought might lead them down a path of thinking things like, "If I use AI to check my logic for flaws after I've drafted my essay, I'll learn more than if I just have it write the essay for me." Again, this one does require well-trained students! However, it's possible to have this happen even down in the primary school years if the scaffolding is in place.

There are a number of ways that students can use AI to test how effective their thinking is with AI. If you want to go deeper with them, you could consider adapting the following:

- **Learning gain check:** After using AI, students write one sentence explaining what they learned that they couldn't have without AI.
- **Bloom's upgrade:** Students take a basic prompt ("List the causes of...") and rewrite it to target a different Bloom's level ("Compare the causes of... and evaluate which was most significant"). We look at this in more detail in Chapter 5, so don't panic!
- **Swap the tool:** Instead of using it for generating content, students use AI for feedback, error-spotting, or counter-arguments that can test how effective their own thinking has been.

* * *

By slowing students down before they type their first word into AI, you get them thinking critically at the point where it matters most: the input. This is where the opportunity lies to shape the whole trajectory of their work. The prompt they choose—and whether they decide to use AI at all—will set boundaries, determine focus, and influence the quality of every piece of thinking that follows.

It's not about fancy prompt engineering or giving students enormous prompts that have been manufactured to 'be the best'. When we teach students to design better prompts, we're helping them to cultivate habits of mind that stick well beyond AI use. Students who learn to pause, clarify, and deliberately choose their next step are learning to regulate their own thinking. They're learning to weigh up whether a tool serves their purpose or derails it. They're learning to interrogate their own assumptions before they commit them to words.

In practical terms, this means normalising a few simple behaviours in the classroom:

- Interrogating the task before interrogating the AI, making sure students know what success looks like in any activity before they seek help or support from an AI tool.
- Iterating on prompts deliberately, testing and refining to see how subtle changes affect the answers.
- Being okay with switching around how and why you might be using AI mid-task, moving from idea generation to critical challenge, or from fact-finding to style-checking.

And while these habits start in AI interactions, they spill over into every other research, writing, or problem-solving task. A student who can frame a thoughtful prompt for an AI can also frame a thoughtful question for a peer, a teacher, or even themselves.

For teachers, this means resisting the temptation to focus only on 'what the AI said' and building in moments where students stop to think, *Why am I asking it this? Is there another way? How might I get better thinking out of it—or out of myself?* You're not just teaching them to use a tool; you're teaching them to think *alongside* the tool, to take ownership of its role in their learning.

3

Thinking critically about AI output

So, your student has generated something with AI. They've thought critically about what they're putting into the tool and if they really need to be using it in the first place.

What comes next?

Remember that any AI tool is just a fancy (okay... *very* fancy) text generator. This means that regardless of whether you're a teacher or student, whether you're generating the text or reading text someone else has generated, you need to think critically about it. When looking at AI output in particular, there are a number of things to encourage your students to consider:

1. Accuracy, errors, and hallucinations
2. Relevance
3. Bias
4. Depth
5. Originality
6. Clarity

7. Sources
8. Ethical concerns

You might look at all of them in one task, or decide there are specific elements that you'd prefer to look at, building skills across all areas over the school year. Let's dig into each of these a little more, and take a look at the types of thinking routines you might use in a classroom context.

1) Accuracy, Errors, and Hallucinations

When we talk about accuracy in AI output, we mean whether the information the AI provides is actually correct and factually reliable. This might sound obvious, but it's especially important because AI tools don't 'know' facts the way humans do. They generate responses based on patterns in data, not on understanding or checking truth. Sometimes, they make mistakes or invent information. This goes for references, too; in the early days of ChatGPT in education, I remember seeing esteemed professors talking about people who would email them and ask for a copy of a paper they'd ostensibly written that ChatGPT had recommended for them. The professor would wrack their brain trying to remember the paper, because by all accounts it was a good one, referenced clearly by the AI and certainly seeming like something they would write. Only... it *wasn't.* ChatGPT had completely hallucinated it.

The Stanford Center for Research on Foundation Models (CRFM) found that the most popular AI tools including those by OpenAI, Anthropic, and Meta have hallucination rates from 3% to 27% depending on how the tool is used. That means there's a large risk to our students of being faced with inaccurate, yet believable, information, and for them to take it at face value if they're not taught to assess it critically. There are tools out there that ostensibly cite their sources, like Perplexity or Google's AI-generated search results, but these are still prone to hallucinations, taking things our of context, or flat-out inaccuracy. An AI might confidently state that a historical figure was born in the wrong year, cite a law that doesn't exist, or make up a quote. That's where critical thinking needs to come in.

Critical thinking is, at its heart, about not taking information at face value. It's *thinking* about it. One of the most fundamental habits of a critical thinker is to ask, "Is this true?" or "How do I know this is correct?" If students accept everything an AI outputs as accurate, they are skipping this essential thinking step. Being able to spot inaccuracies or hallucinations gets our students learning to question, to be sceptical in a healthy way, and to develop a mindset where evidence is always required.

Putting Critical Thinking into Action
Accuracy, Errors, and Hallucinations

1. Use 'spot the error' activities

Give students both accurate and inaccurate AI-generated answers and challenge them to find the mistakes. You can gamify this ('become an AI detective!') to make scepticism a positive habit.

2. Teach verification strategies

Show students how to cross-check AI answers with at least two independent sources, and to look up unfamiliar terms, names, or quotes.

3. Encourage a 'Trust but Verify' attitude

Reinforce that AI can be helpful, but its answers should always be tested, not just trusted. Make it normal for students to be a little sceptical. Remind them that this is the mark of a mature, thoughtful learner.

4. Establish a class routine

After using AI with students, always ask the following questions, and train students to do the same themselves:

- *"Does this sound right?"*
- *"How can we check?"*
- *"What evidence would convince us?"*

5. Model fact-checking out loud

Teachers can demonstrate the process of checking AI outputs against trusted sources (like textbooks, primary sources, or reputable websites). For example:

- *"Let's see if this date matches what's in our textbook."*
- *"The AI says X. Can we find proof of that?"*

2) Relevance

Relevance in the context of AI output means thinking about how well the response actually matches the specific question, task, or purpose at hand.

An AI might produce a detailed, well-written answer, but if it doesn't directly address what was asked, then it isn't truly useful—or, through Willingham's lens, it's not effective. We see this in cases of students handing in AI-generated work with no further thought given to it. Often AI outputs are surface-level or might not cover the specific points that you want students to know (or that you covered in lessons). This can become more of a problem the older a student is and the more specific knowledge they would be expected to have.

For example, if a secondary school student asks *Explain how enzymes are affected by changes in pH and temperature,* the AI might give a general explanation about enzyme structure and function, but fail to address the specific lock-and-key model that was emphasised in their biology class, or miss the practical examples of lactase and pepsin that the teacher used to illustrate optimal pH environments. The answer contains correct information, but doesn't align with the curriculum framework or the specific conceptual models the students are expected to know in their given context.

Relevance also includes whether the output is pitched at the right level (age-appropriate, subject-appropriate), stays on topic, and avoids unnecessary tangents or filler. Sometimes, AI can generate long-winded or generic responses that don't meaningfully engage with the actual assignment or question. Often due to the length, students skim the response and assume it is correct simply because it's long. The appearance of authority strikes again!

Considering this through the lens of critical thinking, determining relevance becomes a time to ask "Does this answer the question?" or "Is this information what I actually need right now?" Accepting a response simply because it looks impressive or is well-phrased is a sign of surface-level thinking. Evaluating relevance requires students to engage more deeply with both the question and the AI's response, clarifying their own goals and standards.

This habit also fosters purposeful learning. Students who are trained to assess relevance become more precise in their research and communication. They avoid being distracted by irrelevant details and develop the ability to sift through information efficiently, which becomes essential as they get older and interact more in our increasingly information-rich society.

Putting Critical Thinking into Action

Relevant Outputs

1. Get students to rephrase the question or task

Before evaluating AI output, have students restate in their own words what they are actually trying to find out or accomplish. This helps them focus on what a relevant answer should include.

2. Practice highlighting or annotating

Teach students to highlight or underline sentences or sections of the AI response that actually answer the question. Anything left un-highlighted may be irrelevant. (And yes, this is likely what you're already teaching even without AI!)

3. Use "Does it Answer the Question?" checks

After generating an AI response, prompt students to explicitly ask:

- *"Is this what I asked for?"*
- *"Which parts directly address my question, and which are off-topic?"*

4. Compare AI responses

As a way to practice this together, give students both relevant and irrelevant AI-generated answers to the same question. Ask them to identify which is better and why. Discuss what makes an answer stray off topic.

5. Encourage precision in prompting

Show students that the relevance of the output often depends on the precision of the input. It's that classic adage again: garbage in, garbage out! Encourage them to ask follow-up questions or to refine their prompts if the answer isn't focused enough.

6. Connect to real-world scenarios

Discuss how in real life (e.g., job interviews, writing reports, solving problems), relevance is often more important than sheer volume of information. Practise evaluating AI outputs in this context to help students understand what you really mean by 'relevance.'

3) Bias

No matter which subjects you teach, checking bias should be an integral part of your practice. From checking (and challenging) bias in materials such as textbooks to ensuring representation for all students, it makes sense that we should also be considering bias in use of AI—both for ourselves and students. In a nutshell, we need to think about how and why AI says what it says. Bias in AI output means that the information, perspective, or language presented is not neutral. It favours certain viewpoints, cultures, or assumptions, often without stating them openly. Bias can show up in many ways: through the examples chosen, the language used, the facts emphasised or omitted, or the underlying worldview reflected in the answer.

A unique challenge with AI is that most large models are trained on vast amounts of internet data, much of which Punya Mishra and other researchers refer to as being produced by and for people in Western, Educated, Industrialised, Rich, Democratic (WEIRD) societies. This can cause AI to reproduce the perspectives, values, and assumptions common in these cultures, sometimes to the exclusion of others. For example, when asked about 'family,' an AI might default to a nuclear family model; when discussing historical events, it may focus on Western sources or interpretations. Bias isn't always obvious—sometimes it's in what's left out, or in small word choices that shape the narrative. This is why bias can be harder to spot than outright errors. It's also why it's so important to be training our students to spot bias in AI output, in the same way we want them to have media literacy and to check bias in more traditional media such as newspapers.

When students learn to check for bias, they become more reflective and sceptical consumers of information. They begin to recognise that 'truth' is often shaped by context, power, and culture. Awareness of

WEIRD bias is crucial in a global classroom. Students should know that AI may not represent the perspectives of non-Western societies, minority groups, or those outside mainstream narratives. This makes checking for bias not just an academic skill, but a matter of fairness, representation, and justice.

Putting Critical Thinking into Action

Dealing with Biased Outputs

1. Teach students to ask, "whose voice is this?"

Encourage students to look for whose perspective is being represented—and whose is not. Ask:

- *"Is this answer only giving one country's or group's viewpoint?"*
- *"What perspectives are missing?"*

2. Discuss WEIRD data and its implications

Explicitly teach students what WEIRD stands for and why it matters in AI.

- *"Let's see how this AI describes 'family' in different countries."*
- *"Does the AI focus mostly on American or European examples? What about the rest of the world?"*

3. Compare multiple sources

Have students look up the same question in different AI tools, or compare AI output to textbooks from other countries or cultural backgrounds.

- *"How does the AI's answer about World War II compare to our textbook? What's similar or different?"*

4. Analyse language and framing

Teach students to examine word choices and implied values in AI output:

- *"Does this answer use words like 'advanced', 'developed', 'primitive', or 'traditional'? What does that imply?"*
- *"Is the language neutral, or does it make judgments?"*

5. Practice filling the gaps

Ask students to imagine or research what perspectives or facts might be missing.

- *"What might someone from a different country, religion, or background say about this topic?"*
- *"Is there a marginalised or less-heard voice not present here?"*

6. Encourage open discussion

Make bias detection a normal, open part of classroom dialogue. Allow students to share when they notice something feels off or one-sided. Celebrate these insights as evidence of good critical thinking!

4) Depth

We've already talked a little about how AI often defaults to surface-level responses rather than one with any depth involved. A deep answer goes beyond surface details or a simple list of facts; it explains, analyses, and sometimes connects ideas or perspectives.

Depth can involve exploring causes and consequences, considering multiple viewpoints, making connections to broader themes, or providing examples and evidence. By contrast, the shallow responses that you might get from AI could be generic, repetitive, or overly simplistic as it is likely trained to provide safe, average responses. As a result, its output can be superficial, especially if the prompt isn't specific or challenging.

For example, an AI-generated answer for an English writing class might state that *The author uses imagery, metaphor, and symbolism to convey the protagonist's emotional journey* without actually analysing specific passages, explaining how these literary devices work together to create meaning, or connecting them to the writer's broader themes or historical context. Even though the AI answer is technically correct in identifying literary devices, it lacks the analytical depth and textual engagement that demonstrates genuine literary understanding and critical thinking.

Depth in the context of critical thinking in AI therefore means we're looking at how to make sense of facts, not just knowing them; making sense of information, seeing connections, asking 'why' and 'how,' and recognising complexity. Or to put it more simply, it's about... *thinking.*

Putting Critical Thinking into Action

Going to Greater Depth

1. Teach students to distinguish between shallow and deep answers

Show students examples of both superficial and deep responses (from AI or human sources). Discuss what makes one answer more substantial than another.

- *"Is this answer just listing facts, or does it explain, analyse, or connect ideas?"*
- *"Does it provide reasons, examples, or evidence?"*

2. Use probing questions

Encourage students to push for more depth by asking 'why?', 'how?', 'so what?', or 'what's the evidence?' After reading an AI output, get them to ask:

- *"Why did that happen?"*
- *"How do we know?"*
- *"What is the impact or consequence?"*

You could even ask this yourself in front of the class! Not sure how? Skip forward to Chapter 7 for a deep dive into this style of think aloud.

3. Encourage Multi-Perspective Analysis

Have students look for whether the AI considers more than one viewpoint or possibility. This is also helpful when used in conjunction with activities that can support with understanding bias.

- *"Does this answer mention only one side?"*
- *"What else could be included to show deeper understanding?"*

4. Get students to practice adding depth

Set tasks where students must take a shallow AI answer and expand it by adding explanation, analysis, examples, or connections to other topics.

5. Provide depth AI checklists

Give students a simple set of questions to ask themselves:

1. *Does the answer explain reasons, not just state facts?*
2. *Are examples or evidence included?*
3. *Does it link ideas or show cause and effect?*
4. *Does it consider more than one perspective?*

6. Scaffold deeper prompts

Teach students to give AI more complex, open-ended prompts. For example, instead of "What caused the French Revolution?", try "Explain the most significant causes of the French Revolution and how they affected different groups in society."

5) Originality

AI tools are designed to generate 'safe,' average content based on the patterns they've seen in their training data. As a result, their output often sounds generic or formulaic unless prompted to do otherwise. This can lead to answers that feel bland, predictable, or copy-pasted from what's most common in the materials it was trained on (which themselves are probably, as we've noted, already WEIRD).

In comparison, an original answer brings something new to the table. That's what makes human responses to anything so unique; we bring a surprising perspective, a thoughtful connection, or a personal insight. Students need to think critically about AI output, therefore, so they don't just end up repeating well-worn facts or phrases, and can instead contribute something that shows individual thought or goes beyond the obvious.

Critical thinking is about more than just finding the 'right' answer; it's about making your own meaning, asking new questions, and developing your own voice. Originality is a key marker of deeper engagement with a topic, as it shows that the student isn't just accepting what's given, but is willing to take intellectual risks, try new approaches, or synthesise ideas in unexpected ways.

When students accept AI output without adding their own twist or insight, they miss the chance to exercise creativity and personal agency. In all honesty, they miss the chance to have fun with learning! Encouraging originality helps students move from passive consumers of information to active, independent thinkers.

Putting Critical Thinking into Action

Fostering Originality with AI

1. Compare for 'sameness'

Have students look for signs of generic content in AI outputs:

- *"Does this sound like something anyone could have written?"*
- *"Is there anything in this answer that surprises me or makes me think differently?"*

2. Encourage personal connections

Ask students to relate the AI's output to their own experiences, opinions, or local context.

- *"Can I add an example from my own life or community that the AI didn't mention?"*
- *"How does my perspective differ from what the AI says?"*

3. Set tasks that require synthesis or creativity

Give assignments that can't be answered by simple summarisation, for example:

- *"Combine two different historical perspectives to create your own argument."*
- *"Suggest a new solution to a problem based on what you've learned."*

4. Be deliberate: prompt for uniqueness

Teach students to prompt AI for original ideas. Note that AI's role as a text generator means the ideas may not be genuinely unique, but this could be a nice way to get more than the generic first response.

- *"Give me an unusual example of..."*
- *"What is a lesser-known viewpoint on...?"*

5. Ask for multiple responses

Instead of asking for a single response, ask the AI tool to generate 5-10 responses and get students to take the best parts from each one.

6. Practice editing for voice

Encourage students to rewrite AI output in their own words, adding their own humour, style, or insights. This helps them develop their own authorial voice and see where AI is bland or generic.

6) Clarity

When we talk about clarity, what we're talking about is how clear something is to understand. A clear answer is well-organised, uses straightforward language, and explains ideas in a way that makes sense to its intended audience. That means clarity might look different for different age groups or in different subject areas, because it means something different depending on context. Clarity also means avoiding jargon, ambiguity, or overly complex sentences that might confuse the reader.

Note that this doesn't mean you have to always use simple language to be considered clear! The latest research in a peer-reviewed academic journal, for example, is expected to be delivered with clarity. However, it is also expected to include subject-specific jargon and a certain level of complexity as is suited for its intended audience. It's clarity, but for people who might have a different average understanding to your typical high school student.

In comparison, AI-generated outputs sometimes produce sentences that sound complicated, use unfamiliar vocabulary, or jump between ideas without clear transitions, with no real consideration for its audience unless explicitly prompted—and even then, it might not get things right! An AI response often gives the illusion of clarity, but the more you look into it the more you realise that actually there's no clarity at all.

AI tools have what's called a 'context window'. This is the amount of text that you can input into an AI tool before it loses track of its knowledge base. If you use the same chat thread for a long time, you might find that the AI becomes less clear the more it is used. It may even begin to contradict itself or use terms incorrectly.

This can make answers hard to follow, especially for students working at different reading levels or for whom English is an additional language. And of course, it makes it clear that the work is largely AI-written, particularly when the student themselves can't explain the point they're trying to get across.

Evaluating clarity helps students become more active readers and listeners. Rather than pretending to understand or skipping over difficult parts, they can act as critical thinkers, stopping to ask, "What does this mean?". When a student is able to evaluate the clarity of something, they look for gaps in logic, unclear terms, or muddled explanations and try to resolve them. This habit is essential both for working with AI and for more 'traditional skills' such as understanding textbooks, lectures, and peer discussions.

Putting Critical Thinking into Action

Ensuring Clarity

1. Encourage active reading and listening

Teach students to read (or listen to) AI outputs with a questioning mindset.

- *"Do I really understand every part of this?"*
- *"Are there words, phrases, or ideas that aren't clear to me?"*

2. Highlight or annotate confusing sections

Have students underline or highlight any parts of the AI response they find confusing, ambiguous, or overly complex. Discuss these as a class or in groups. On the plus side, they might possibly be used to tasks like this already, so the new element is the AI of it all, rather than an entirely new task.

3. Paraphrase for understanding

Ask students to restate parts of the AI output in their own words. If they struggle, that's a sign the original wasn't clear. They might want to ask the AI to simplify the output to suit them better, or you could guide them to use other tools at their disposal.

- *"Can you explain this sentence to a friend?"*
- *"How would you say this more simply?"*

4. Encourage questions

Create a routine where students are expected to ask for clarification whenever something isn't clear:

- *"What does this word mean?"*
- *"Can the AI explain this in another way?"*

5. Teach the use of follow-up prompts

Show students how to prompt the AI for clarification:

- *Explain [X] in simpler terms*
- *Give an example of [X] that links to [student interest]*
- *What does [unfamiliar word] mean? Put it in a sentence and give me a simple definition.*
- *Explain this in language for a [X]-year-old student*

6. Compare multiple outputs

Have students generate the same answer at different reading levels, or using different prompt styles. Discuss which is clearest and why.

7. Model clear communication

Demonstrate how to break down complex ideas into step-by-step explanations. When giving feedback, praise clarity in both student writing and AI outputs.

7) Sources

In academic work, credible sources are essential for verifying facts, supporting arguments, and showing where information comes from. With AI, the challenge is that it doesn't typically cite specific sources unless you specifically request it to do so; instead, it generates answers based on patterns learned from huge datasets (websites, books, articles) during its training. As mentioned earlier in this chapter, AI may attempt to provide references, but these can be made up ('hallucinated') or be vague and untraceable.

Knowing the provenance of a fact or quotation is critical for judging its reliability, relevance, and authority. Without clear sourcing, students can't easily check if information is trustworthy or up to date, nor can they check for bias or work towards a more well-rounded perspective. Accepting claims without knowing their origins opens the door to misinformation, misunderstanding, and weak arguments. Checking sources is therefore a core academic habit and a vital real-world skill.

AI's lack of transparent sourcing is a unique challenge—and that goes even for AI tools that purport to link to information sources, with some still taking their information out of context. This means students must be even more vigilant about verifying facts, cross-checking claims, and understanding that just because something 'sounds right,' doesn't mean it's accurate or trustworthy.

Putting Critical Thinking into Action

AI and Source Checking

1. Make source-checking a routine task

Even in subjects where source analysis isn't necessarily the norm, encourage students to always ask:

- *"Where does this information come from?"*
- *"Did the AI invent sources? How can I check?"*

2. Teach verification skills

Show students how to:

- Look up key facts, quotes, or data from the AI output in textbooks, reputable websites, or academic articles.
- Use online search tools, databases, or physical resources to check if a citation or statistic is real. Alongside this, teach how to check whether a given website is reliable or not.

3. Encourage the use of multiple sources

Train students not to rely solely on AI for information. Have them compare AI answers with other materials and highlight where sources agree or differ.

4. Model good practice

Whenever you use AI in class, model your own process of checking for sources and confirming information before accepting or using it.

5. Assign source-finding tasks

Ask students to take a claim from AI and find the original source, or to annotate an AI-generated answer with references they found themselves to back up the assertion.

8) Ethical Concerns

A simple definition of ethics is that it's anything to do with right and wrong, fairness, harm, and respect for others. Something that is perhaps a little bit more unique to AI than to other methods of finding information (although perhaps not entirely so!) is the types of ethical considerations you meet when using it—both before and after input. These include:

- **Privacy**: Does the AI output include or request personal or sensitive information?
- **Copyright/Plagiarism**: Is the AI copying the work of others without acknowledgment? Are images, text, or data used without proper permissions?
- **Harmful Content**: Does the output contain, support, or normalise stereotypes, prejudice, hate, violence, or misinformation?

- **Sensitivity**: Does it touch on difficult or distressing topics in an insensitive way?
- **Authenticity**: Is it honest about what it is and where the information comes from? Is it pretending to be a person or expert when it's not?
- **Appropriateness**: Is the content suitable for the audience and context, or could it cause offence or misunderstanding?
- **Manipulation**: Is the AI being used to deceive or influence unfairly (e.g., fake reviews, deepfakes, or 'sock puppet' accounts)?

AI may not 'intend' harm, but biased data, careless prompting, or misuse can produce ethically questionable output. In the context of critical thinking, that means students need to think not only about what is true or useful about what the AI gives them, but also about what is right and responsible. When students evaluate AI output ethically, they practise empathy, responsibility, and social awareness. They learn to consider the impact of information on themselves, others, and wider society.

This is especially important with AI, which can quickly scale up harm (e.g., spreading stereotypes or fake news) or make it easy to cut corners (e.g., copying work, not citing sources).

Putting Critical Thinking into Action

Ethical AI Usage

1. Discuss real-life scenarios

Present examples where AI output could cause harm, break rules, or offend. Discuss:

- *"Is it okay to use AI to write your homework and submit it as your own?"*
- *"What if an AI-generated image uses someone's face without permission?"*
- *"What if AI gives an answer that stereotypes a group of people?"*

2. Teach an ethics check routine

Encourage students to always pause and ask:

1. *"Could this output hurt anyone?"*
2. *"Does it respect privacy and copyright?"*
3. *"Is this honest and fair?"*

3. Teach about plagiarism and attribution

Make clear that copying AI-generated work and passing it off as your own is still plagiarism if not acknowledged. Show how to cite or reference AI use where appropriate. Many exam boards or school groups have their own guidance on how and when to cite

AI use. Ensure you're teaching the appropriate one to suit your context.

4. Encourage empathy and perspective-taking

Ask students to consider:

- *"How might someone else feel reading this?"*
- *"Would I want my own information used in this way?"*

5. Model responsible use

Demonstrate your own decision-making as a teacher: when you choose not to use AI for a task, or when you adapt output to avoid harm.

Cognitive Offloading

4

Understanding Cognitive Offloading

It's Sunday morning, which means it's probably time to plan your meals for the week. Here's your to do list for the day:

- Check what food you already have and what you need to order more of
- Think about what's on the calendar and how that might impact how much time (if any) you'll have to cook
- Check what specials might be available in the various flyers that are piled up on your kitchen bench
- Consider what little treats you should probably sneak into the basket to get you through the week...

Once everything is ticked off, it's time to head to the supermarket, where you are faced with an enormous display of your favourite chocolates (on special, no less!) and you promptly forget everything you planned to buy.

Oh wait—no you don't... because you made a shopping list!

Even though it sounds fancy on the surface, that's all cognitive offloading is: offloading your thinking to an external storage system, be it digital or analogue. When you go to the supermarket, you don't have to try and remember your shopping list. Instead, you write it down. You offload your thinking process to your notebook—or to the notes app on your phone.

The fact that we have exercise books where students write down their learning rather than having to remember it all? That's another form of cognitive offloading. You can almost imagine Plato rolling his eyes at our modern reliance on notebooks; he wasn't exactly thrilled about the written word replacing memory. How about another common example of cognitive offloading that I've used a lot in my own classroom: letting students make a 'cheat sheet' by taking an index card and writing everything they needed on there before they go in for a test or assessment. One more that again you might be aware of: when I was at school doing physics, we'd get a little sheet with certain formulae on it. I didn't have to remember those formulae during the exam; I could focus on putting them into action instead. The cognitive load was shifted from memorisation to application.

So cognitive offloading isn't new. Not by a long shot.

Researchers define cognitive offloading as occurring when people reduce their mental load by deploying actions that change the demands of a task. In other words, cognitive offloading is a way to not have to continually hold a thought in your mind, therefore freeing your brain up to think about something else. There are three different types of offloading that are particularly relevant when we start to think about this in the context of education:

- External normalisation
- Intentional offloading

- Transactive memory systems

Understanding that there are different types of cognitive offloading helps us see that cognitive offloading isn't inherently good or bad, and that it depends on what type you're doing and for what purpose. Let's take a minute to dig into each of these types of cognitive offloading and put them into context of what's happening in your classroom right now, before we step into the AI of it all.

External Normalisation

External normalisation is when you physically arrange your environment or tools to make thinking easier or reduce the cognitive load of a task. Think about the following examples you might already see students using in your classroom:

- **Highlighting key passages** in a textbook so students don't have to remember where to find important information within a larger piece. This also creates 'visual landmarks' which help the brain to quickly recognise highlighted sections without having to process the meaning of surrounding text.
- **Using different coloured pens** for different subjects or types of notes. The brain can immediately identify a subject or topic without reading the content first, and as visual patterns are processed faster than text, students can navigate their notes more quickly.
- **Putting sticky notes on specific pages** of a book they need to reference for an essay. Students don't need to remember, "the quote I need is on page 47" while also formulating arguments,

and it means they can jump between ideas physically rather than mentally, which is less mentally taxing.

- **Using graphic organisers or mind maps** to visually structure their thinking. Visual structure helps the brain understand relationships between ideas without having to constantly remember what connects to what. Students are essentially creating an external version of their internal thought processes, which allows them to 'think bigger' than their working memory would normally allow.
- **Setting up their laptop with multiple tabs open** for research so they don't lose track of sources (like me writing this book, for example!). This way, students don't forget where they found information. They can quickly switch between sources to compare information without holding details in memory and create a visual-spatial organisation of information.

External normalisation is generally a 'safe' form of cognitive offloading because students are still doing the thinking—they're just making it easier for their brains to manage. When we see students using highlighters or making revision cards, they're engaging in external normalisation, and it usually enhances rather than replaces their thinking.

Intentional Offloading

Intentional offloading is when you create external systems to remind you to do something later, so you don't have to keep holding that information in your working memory right now. For me, that's setting an alarm to remind me to take the bins out every night...

For your students, this might look like:

- **Writing homework assignments in their planner** so they don't have to remember them. This frees up working memory for learning, instead of using it to remember what homework they should be thinking. It also reduces the constant low-level worry of "Am I forgetting something?" which consumes cognitive resources even when students aren't consciously aware of it.
- **Creating to-do lists** for multi-step projects. Breaking large projects into visible steps makes them feel more manageable and less cognitively intimidating, and means the brain can focus on one step at a time rather than trying to juggle the entire project mentally. Plus, checking off completed items gives a sense of accomplishment that results in continued motivation!
- **Bookmarking websites** they need to return to for research. This means there's no need to remember or reconstruct search strategies that led to useful sources. It also allows students to follow interesting tangents without fear of losing their main research thread.

Similarly to external normalisation, intentional offloading is also a relatively safe form of cognitive offloading in the educational sense because it's about task management, not thinking replacement. In fact, when students get better at this type of offloading, they often become better learners because they're not constantly worried about forgetting things. Their cognitive resources are freed up for actual learning rather than administrative tasks.

Transactive Memory Systems

Finally, there are transactive memory systems. These are when you rely on other people (or technology) to remember certain types of information because you know you can access it when needed. You don't store the information yourself—you store knowledge about where to find it. In other words, it's like writing down that grocery list rather than trying to remember it.

That might look like:

- **Knowing that the teacher always puts key dates on the whiteboard or your LMS**, so students don't memorise the actual dates but know where to look for them. Students learn to remember where information is rather than the information itself, which is often more efficient, and they can trust that the information will be there when needed, reducing anxiety about forgetting. However, students sacrifice some independence (they need to be in that classroom / on that website to access the information) in exchange for cognitive efficiency and reduced memory load.
- **Understanding that certain types of information are always in the textbook appendix**. This helps develop 'meta-knowledge' about information sources: students learn not just facts, but where different types of facts live. It also speeds up problem solving, as it means they can quickly access formulas, conversion tables, or definitions without interrupting their thinking flow. However, this does mean that students must develop and maintain knowledge about the structure and organisation of their resources.
- **Relying on their partner** to remember the steps of experimental procedures while they focus on observations. Each partner can excel in their area of strength rather than trying to do everything adequately, meaning students don't have to constantly shift between procedural memory and observational attention. The

partnership develops capabilities that neither individual could achieve alone, although it does run the risk that students become dependent on their partner and may not develop full procedural competence.

- **Knowing the best websites to find certain information on** (a bit like me knowing that *Wookiepedia* is where I should go for all my esoteric Star Wars knowledge...). This develops 'source expertise', where students become skilled at matching information needs with optimal sources. Instead of trying multiple sources, students can go directly to the most reliable and comprehensive option, and in turn this creates efficient workflows where students develop systematic approaches to information gathering.

Transactive memory systems are where things can get a little tricky. You can see this even in the bullet points above which, unlike the first two types of cognitive offloading, each come with caveats.

* * *

Before we go any further, I want us to quickly take a look at five key points that research tells us about how and why cognitive offloading takes place. That way, we'll have a firmer understanding of where we're going next.

Key Finding 1: Learners with lower working memory capacity tend to offload more information

Working memory is where you hold and manipulate information *while* you're thinking, before it goes into more permanent storage. Some students naturally have more working memory capacity than others. Students with smaller working memory 'tanks' are more likely to use external tools (including AI) to store information. This isn't about intelligence so much as cognitive architecture. These students aren't being lazy when they reach for external supports; they're being strategic. In fact, when they offload appropriately, they often perform just as well as students with higher working memory capacity.

Key Finding 2: Learners with lower perceived working memory capacity offload more information

This one isn't just about actual working memory capacity, but about how much capacity students think they have. Students who believe they have poor memory or who might get overwhelmed easily are more likely to offload, regardless of their actual cognitive abilities. This suggests that confidence and self-perception play huge roles in offloading decisions. Sometimes students who could handle more cognitive load choose not to because they don't believe in their own capabilities.

Key Finding 3: Higher extraneous cognitive load triggers offloading

Extraneous cognitive load refers to mental effort that's not directly related to learning the main concept—things like confusing instructions, poorly designed materials, or distracting environments. When students are dealing with high extraneous load, they're more likely to offload other thinking tasks. This is actually a positive thing! It shows students making smart decisions about where to focus their limited cognitive resources. When the environment is creating unnecessary cognitive demands, strategic offloading can preserve mental energy for what matters.

Key Finding 4: Higher intrinsic cognitive load leads to more offloading

Intrinsic cognitive load is the mental effort directly required by the learning material itself—how complex or difficult the core concept is. When students are grappling with genuinely difficult ideas, they're more likely to offload peripheral tasks. This is strategic and appropriate! When core concepts are demanding, it makes sense to offload ancillary tasks. The key is ensuring students are offloading the right things and supporting tasks rather than the core learning itself.

Key Finding 5: Higher perceived value of information prompts learners to invest more effort in memorisation

When students believe information is really important or valuable, they're more likely to commit it to memory rather than offloading it. Their perception of value drives their offloading decisions. This highlights the crucial role of helping students understand why information is valuable. When we make the importance clear, students will naturally choose to internalise rather than offload.

* * *

That's not to say that there aren't risks. Externally offloading cognition can affect your cognition and does have negative aspects on your memory.

Some studies show that you can feel like you've learnt something when you've offloaded it, even though you haven't actually learnt it. Or, even worse, that your offloaded memories can actually be manipulated. One group of researchers led on a particularly telling study where participants offloaded their thinking to an external digital store. Then researchers changed the file, and participants just didn't notice—they assumed they'd remembered wrong and that the digital file was the real thing. Luckily this risk can be reduced if you let people know that external storage is unreliable. But it does show us that we need to be aware not only of *what* we're offloading, but the risks of it, too.

Studies also consistently show that searching the internet means you're memorising less and makes you think you've learnt the information when you haven't. In fact, you can describe the internet as a 'supernormal stimulus'—an unprecedented form of extended memory that is better than any of the others out there. It lets you do so much that there's a danger of people overestimating their skills and abilities.

It's almost like a digital placebo effect, where the presence of the tool makes you feel more capable than you actually are.

So what can we do about it?

5

When is it Okay to Offload?

So when is it acceptable to let AI do the thinking, if ever? To be honest, I don't know that any of us have the answers. However, one way we could classify beneficial versus harmful cognitive offloading is by linking it to Bloom's Taxonomy. I know that Bloom's can be a contentious topic with multiple perspectives and understandings. However, it can serve as a common leaping off point for us to think about, well, thinking!

For each element of Bloom's, we're going to look at the verbs that often accompanies them, alongside a list of verbs that could be used while prompting AI, before finally looking at what different types of cognitive offloading might look like in the context of that Bloom's level.

Throughout this chapter, I've included a number of thinking routines that can help you to get students (or yourself!) thinking more about what thinking with AI looks like at each level of Bloom's taxonomy. Thinking routines are simple, structured strategies that help students develop and express their thinking more clearly, and I believe the term was first popularised by folk working on Harvard's Project Zero. Some of the more common ones you may have come across include *Think-Pair-Share* or *See-Think-Wonder.* Typically consisting of a short series of steps or prompts such as *What do you notice? What do you wonder?*, these routines encourage students to observe carefully, reflect critically, and engage thoughtfully with learning content. They are valuable to teachers because they promote metacognition, support deeper understanding, and provide a consistent structure for classroom dialogue. Thinking routines can be easily implemented across subjects and age groups by integrating them into daily lessons; as part of discussions, reflections, or responses to new material. The thinking routines in this chapter aren't aimed at being a daily or even weekly activity. Rather, think of them as ways you can support students at whatever part of the learning journey they might be at.

* * *

Remembering

***Remembering* Verbs:** cite, define, describe, identify, label, list, match, name, outline, quote, recall, report, reproduce, retrieve, show, state, tabulate, and tell.

Prompting AI for *Remembering*: remind me of, help me recall, list for me, define, identify, show me, retrieve, find, locate, extract, summarise key facts, provide definitions, generate flashcards, create memory aids, quiz me on, test my recall of, give me examples of, outline, turn into a table, reproduce, display, present, organise by category, sort chronologically, filter by topic, highlight key points.

Remembering & External Normalisation

Using AI for external normalisation means students use it to modify and organise their information environment to make facts more accessible and memorable. When students ask AI to create structured study materials like timelines of historical events, they're modifying their study environment by transforming scattered information into visually organised formats that support better recall.

Similarly, asking AI to generate organised vocabulary lists by theme or to generate formatted reference sheets with key formulae represents external normalisation because students are reshaping how information is presented to them.

They could use AI to create visual aids such as charts comparing different scientific concepts, converting abstract information into concrete visual representations, or ask AI to format their own notes or create templates for organising factual information, again modifying their own notes to make the information more accessible and quicker to understand.

Though this is a relatively simple use of AI at this level, students need to make sure they're focusing on learning the information that they're organising. Otherwise, they run the risk of creating beautifully organised study materials without actually internalising the information, leading to surface-level familiarity rather than genuine recall ability.

Encouraging Effective External Normalisation

- **Model the process:** Demonstrate how to use AI to reorganise information you already understand, not to learn new content.

- **Focus on format, not content:** Encourage AI use for visual organisation, templates, and formatting while students provide the actual information.
- **Build in reflection:** After AI helps organise materials, require students to explain the content in their own words to ensure comprehension.

Remembering & Intentional Offloading

On the other hand, intentional offloading with AI focuses on using AI to create systems that will prompt future recall of information without taking up too much working memory in the present time. For example, when students ask AI to generate practice quizzes for factual content, they're setting up future testing situations that will remind them of information they need to know, offloading the need to remember when and how to review.

Creating personalised revision schedules based on upcoming deadlines also represents intentional offloading because students are programming future reminders about what to study and when, removing the cognitive burden of tracking their own revision needs.

Encouraging Purposeful Intentional Offloading

- **Emphasise student design:** Students should design their own quiz questions and revision schedules, using AI only for formatting and delivery.
- **Build metacognitive awareness:** Regularly discuss when and why to use external reminders versus developing internal memory strategies.

- **Create accountability measures:** Check that AI-generated practice materials actually improve student performance on assessments.

Remembering & Transactive Memory Systems

The most problematic form of cognitive offloading at the remember level—and, as you'll see soon, at most levels—is found when students offload the act of memorising AI.

Remember that this one is about creating a relationship with the AI where they know (or at least, assume) that AI can reliably store and retrieve certain types of information, much in the way they rely on tools like Google to answer their quick questions. When students learn to ask AI for historical dates, scientific constants, or mathematical formulae, they're offloading their memory by establishing AI as a reliable partner for specific types of factual information. This becomes a transactive memory system because students learn what AI knows well, how to access that knowledge effectively, and when to rely on this external source versus their own memory. They could also use AI to verify what they know, plugging in their understanding of facts and asking them if it's correct. Again, this means they run the risk of both hallucinations and sycophancy (where AI just answers in a way that makes them feel good, even to their detriment).

This 'Google effect', where they know how to find information but don't know the information itself, becomes particularly pronounced when students develop reflexive dependence on AI for basic recall. In other words, it's a problem if students automatically reach for AI support even for information they could reasonably be expected to remember, losing confidence in their own memory capabilities.

This creates a concerning pattern where students doubt their own cognitive abilities and become unnecessarily dependent on external tools for routine intellectual tasks. The cognitive effort involved in recalling information from memory is crucial for building knowledge and for strengthening neural connections in the brain, and AI that eliminates this effort entirely can actually impede learning.

Preventing Problematic Transactive Memory Systems

- **Establish AI-free times/zones:** Designate specific times, assignments, or assessments where students must rely on their own memory
- **Practice recall without AI:** Regular low-stakes quizzes and memory exercises that cannot involve AI consultation
- **Address cognitive confidence:** Explicitly discuss how over-reliance on AI can erode confidence in one's own memory abilities
- **Model appropriate boundaries:** Demonstrate when it's reasonable to look something up versus when you should know it from memory

Thinking Routine #1
Before AI - During AI - After AI (B-D-A)

The purpose of this thinking routine is to create a consistent habit of intentional AI use with clear reflection points. This thinking routine works really well when used in conjunction with the metacognitive cycle.

BEFORE AI (2-3 minutes): Students write down:

- What I already know about this topic
- What specific help I need
- What thinking I want to keep for myself
- My success criteria: How will I know if AI helped me learn?

DURING AI (ongoing): Students pause every few minutes to ask:

- Is this what I actually needed?
- Do I understand what the AI is telling me?
- Am I staying in charge of the thinking?

AFTER AI (3-4 minutes): Students reflect:

- What did I learn that I couldn't have learned alone?
- What would I do differently next time?
- Can I teach this to someone else without reading the AI output?
- What thinking did I preserve as 'human-only'?

Understanding

***Understanding* Verbs:** abstract, arrange, articulate, associate, categorise, clarify, classify, compare, compute, conclude, contrast, defend, diagram, differentiate, discuss, distinguish, estimate, exemplify, explain, extend, extrapolate, generalise, give examples of, illustrate, infer, interpolate, interpret, match, outline, paraphrase, predict, rearrange, reorder, rephrase, represent, restate, summarise, transform, translate.

Prompting AI for *Understanding*: explain to me, help me understand, clarify, break down, simplify, illustrate with examples, compare and contrast, show me the relationship between, translate into simpler terms, paraphrase, summarise the key points, give me analogies for, demonstrate how, extrapolate from this data, categorise these concepts, differentiate between, make connections between.

Understanding & External Normalisation

Students can reduce their cognitive load when trying to understand something new by modifying how information is presented to help them understand it better. A simple example is using AI to create a concept map showing relationships between ideas: the student is modifying their information environment to make abstract connections more visible and concrete.

Similarly, asking AI to translate complex academic language into simpler terms or requesting multiple analogies for difficult concepts means students are reshaping their information environment to make abstract ideas more accessible to their current understanding level.

Think of it this way: students could do all these things without AI, but they're using AI to reduce cognitive load in these areas, freeing up working memory to do the actual understanding.

Encouraging Positive External Normalisation

- **Provide the content first:** Ensure students have foundational knowledge before using AI to reorganise or simplify information
- **Require active engagement:** After AI creates concept maps or analogies, students must explain the connections in their own words
- **Check for understanding:** Regularly verify that students comprehend the underlying concepts, not just the AI-generated representations

Understanding & Intentional Offloading

This involves students using AI to create external supports that will later prompt their understanding. For example, they might ask AI to generate summary sheets of key concepts, setting up prompts that help jog their memory in future situations without having to reconstruct their understanding from scratch.

Creating study guides that outline main ideas and supporting details also represents intentional offloading because students are establishing external memory aids that prompt them to remember not just facts, but how concepts connect. However, it's important to monitor how much students rely on AI for these study guides—there's a risk that they might mistake AI-generated explanations for their own understanding.

When learning involves only passive consumption of AI-created concept maps or graphic organisers without students doing the cognitive work of making sense of relationships themselves, comprehension remains superficial. Students may feel they understand because they've seen well-organised information, but they haven't actually internalised the learning. Not true, and yet very common!

Supporting Strategic Intentional Offloading

- **Student-generated content first:** Require students to create initial summaries or concept connections before using AI to enhance them
- **Process over product:** Focus assessment on students' ability to explain their thinking, not the quality of AI-generated study materials
- **Create understanding checkpoints:** Use frequent informal assessments to ensure AI study aids actually improve comprehension
- **Emphasise personal meaning-making:** Help students connect new concepts to their prior knowledge and experiences

Understanding & Transactive Memory Systems

Once again, we encounter our familiar friend-turned-nemesis: transactive memory systems. Don't get me wrong, there are some good uses of this type of cognitive offloading at this level, too!

When students learn to ask AI for different explanations of the same concept until they find one that clicks, they're offloading their memory by taking advantage of AI's ability to provide multiple perspectives on complex ideas.

Students might use AI to check their understanding by explaining concepts in their own words and asking for feedback on accuracy; this is a form of transactive memory systems because they're using AI as a partner for verifying their own understanding. Through doing this, they might actually develop a level of expertise in knowing when to ask AI for background context, alternative explanations, or clarifying examples versus when they need to work through challenges independently.

All of these are great skills to have for an AI-powered future, however it becomes problematic when students consistently rely on AI to explain concepts rather than wrestling with understanding themselves.

While AI can provide helpful explanations, students who immediately turn to AI when encountering difficult material miss the productive struggle that builds genuine comprehension. This creates a concerning level of dependence where students doubt their ability to make sense of complex information independently and lose confidence in their own comprehension capabilities. When students rely heavily on AI-generated summaries and study guides without creating their own meaning-making processes, they develop shallow, fragmented understanding rather than coherent conceptual frameworks.

Preventing Problematic Transactive Memory Systems

- **Establish 'struggle zones':** Create specific times when students must work through difficult concepts without AI assistance
- **Teach productive struggle:** Linked to the above, help students recognise that confusion and difficulty are normal parts of deep learning
- **Require explanation before consultation:** Students must attempt to explain concepts themselves before seeking AI clarification
- **Monitor dependency patterns:** Watch for students who reflexively turn to AI rather than engaging with challenging content

Thinking Routine #2
GRASP - GAP - GUIDE - GROW

This routine is a helpful step-by-step guide to help students understand and learn how and when to use AI to develop their understanding of a topic.

GRASP: What do I currently understand?

Before any AI interaction, students capture their baseline:

- Write down what you think you understand about this concept/topic
- Identify the main ideas as you currently see them
- Note any connections you can make to things you already know
- Circle or highlight parts you're confident about vs. uncertain about

GAP: Where exactly is my understanding incomplete?

Students then identify specific comprehension gaps:

- What parts make no sense to me?
- Where do I need clearer explanations?
- What connections am I missing?
- Do I need different examples or analogies?
- Am I missing background knowledge?

GUIDE: How can AI be my learning guide?

Students prompt the AI with specific, strategic requests:

- "I understand X and Y, but I'm confused about how Z connects. Can you explain just that relationship?"
- "I need a simpler explanation of [specific concept] - I'm getting lost in the technical language"
- "Can you give me a real-world example of [concept] that's different from [textbook example]?"
- "I think [concept] works like [my explanation]. Is that accurate? What am I missing?"

GROW: How can I deepen and verify my understanding?

Immediately after their AI interaction, students should try some of the following:

- Explain the concept again in their own words (without looking at AI response)
- Create their own example or analogy
- Try to teach it to someone else or write it as if teaching
- Connect it to something else they've learned
- Test their comprehension:
    - Can I apply this understanding to a new situation?
    - What would happen if I changed one variable?
    - How does this connect to the bigger picture?
    - What questions do I still have?
- Document their learning:
    - What did I understand before vs. after AI help?

- Which part of my understanding came from my own thinking vs. AI support?
- What do I still need to work on?

Applying

***Applying* Verbs:** apply, calculate, carry out, classify, complete, compute, demonstrate, dramatise, employ, examine, execute, experiment, generalise, illustrate, implement, infer, interpret, manipulate, modify, operate, organise, outline, predict, solve, transfer, translate, use.

Prompting AI for *Applying*: help me apply, guide me through solving, show me how to use, demonstrate the process of, implement this method in, execute the procedure for, carry out the steps to, modify this example for, adapt this technique to, transfer this concept to, solve this problem using, practice with me, reformat this by, simulate the application of, model how to use, generate practice problems, create scenarios where I can apply, test my application of, provide feedback on my use of.

Applying & External Normalisation

When applying their learning, students can use AI to modify how problems and application tasks are presented, making them seem more 'do-able'. For example, they might ask AI to break complex multi-step problems into smaller, manageable components, restructuring their environment to help them apply learning more systematically.

Students might ask AI to reformat word problems into bullet points or tables to make key information more visible—this one has been particularly common with students I've taught, and to be honest I often do this myself with extended texts to make it easier to focus on what matters! This approach adjusts how information is presented, reducing cognitive load and allowing students to focus on actual application rather than spending excessive time working out what the problem is asking them to do.

Students could even use AI to generate practice problems with varying difficulty levels or contexts. In cognitive offloading terms, they're creating a more supportive practice environment that scaffolds their application skills development.

However, there are significant risks at this level (although let's be honest, at this point when are there *not* risks!). When external normalisation becomes just the AI solving problems step-by-step while students passively follow along, they miss the cognitive work that builds genuine application skills. I've seen this frequently in subjects like maths, where students mistake 'watching AI work through the steps' for 'actually learning the process.'

Encouraging Positive External Normalisation

- **Maintain problem complexity:** Ensure AI simplifies presentation format, not the actual cognitive demands of the task
- **Create interactive AI prompts:** Prompt AI tools to ask guiding questions rather than provide direct solutions, such as in the mathematics example above.
- **Focus on process over format:** Emphasise that clearer presentation should lead to better problem-solving, not passive consumption

Applying & Intentional Offloading

You're hopefully seeing a trend here: intentional offloading is perhaps the most common and often most useful form of cognitive offloading. For application tasks, students can intentionally offload some thinking by setting up external prompts that guide future application without requiring them to memorise every step.

They might ask AI to create step-by-step checklists for complex procedures or set up spaced practice schedules for different application tasks, prompting them to maintain and strengthen their abilities over time.

However, it's important to realise that in doing this, students risk becoming dependent on external supports that won't always be available. The cognitive effort involved in remembering procedures, recognising problem types, and selecting appropriate strategies is crucial for building expertise, so it's important we work on scaffolding *away* from this form of offloading as much as we scaffold how to do it!

Supporting Strategic Intentional Offloading

- **Scaffold independence gradually:** Start with AI-generated checklists, progress to student-created templates, end with independent work
- **Build procedural fluency first:** Ensure students understand processes before creating external supports
- **Monitor dependency patterns:** Watch for students who can't function without their AI-created supports

Applying & Transactive Memory Systems

When applying thinking, patterns of problematic transactive memory systems emerge when students consistently rely on AI to verify every step of their work rather than developing internal confidence in their problem-solving abilities.

While AI can provide useful feedback, students who immediately turn to AI for validation after every decision miss the opportunity to develop problem-solving intuition and self-monitoring skills.

In a more positive version of this type of cognitive offloading, students might instead use AI to explore alternative solution methods after attempting problems themselves, which represents transactive memory systems because they're leveraging AI's knowledge of different approaches while maintaining their own problem-solving responsibility.

When students ask AI to provide feedback on their application strategies or suggest improvements to their problem-solving process, they're engaging in this transactive memory systems by knowing how to use AI's analytical capabilities to enhance their own performance. Students might develop expertise in knowing when to ask AI for hints versus full solutions, or when to request procedural guidance versus conceptual clarification.

Preventing Problematic Transactive Memory Systems

- **Delay verification:** Require students to complete entire problems before seeking AI feedback
- **Build self-monitoring skills:** Teach students to check their own work before turning to AI or other external skills
- **Practice problem recognition:** Train students to identify problem types and select strategies without AI guidance

- **Peer collaboration over AI:** Encourage students to discuss challenges with others before consulting AI

Thinking Routine #3
The Spiral Practice Method

This one is a routine whereby students start at the centre of a spiral (either imagined or drawn) and deepen their approach to skill application with strategic AI support.

Start at the centre: Think about the basics

- What's the core skill or knowledge I need to apply independently?

First spiral out: Try applying it in the simplest possible context

- What's working with my own knowledge? What's not?
- Where might AI help organise my approach without doing the thinking?
- Make one small adjustment based on your own reasoning

Second spiral out: Apply the adjusted approach to a slightly more complex situation

- How does the added complexity change things?
- Could AI help me track multiple variables whilst I focus on problem-solving?
- What new challenges emerge that I need to work through myself?

Third spiral out: Try it in a genuinely new or challenging context

- What breaks down? What transfers well?
- Where might AI provide verification of my steps without replacing my reasoning?
- How do I need to evolve my approach based on what I'm learning?

Spiral back in: Return to the core with enriched understanding

- How has my grasp of the fundamental skill deepened through my own practice?
- What can I now see that I couldn't before?
- How did AI support enhance rather than replace my learning?

Analysing

***Analysing* Verbs:** analyse, appraise, attribute, break down, categorise, compare, contrast, correlate, deconstruct, deduce, differentiate, discriminate, distinguish, examine, experiment, identify, illustrate, infer, inspect, investigate, organise, outline, question, relate, separate, subdivide, test.

Prompting AI for *Analysing*: help me analyse, break down for me, compare the factors of, contrast the aspects of, investigate the relationship between, deconstruct this into parts, separate the key features of, categorise the components, correlate the data points, differentiate between the elements, distinguish the patterns in, outline the structure of, question the assumptions in, inspect the evidence for, test the validity of, appraise the significance of, deduce the causes of, relate the parts to the whole, subdivide this concept into.

Analysing & External Normalisation

AI offloading at the analyse level presents significant risks to critical thinking development when used inappropriately. AI use at this level should focus on modifying how complex information is presented to make analytical work more manageable. This could include organising large datasets into tables or charts that highlight patterns, or separating different types of evidence or arguments within a text. Basically, it's anything that allows the brain space to be spent on analysis rather than parsing.

These approaches let students restructure their analytical environment, organising complex information into categories that support systematic analysis while keeping the actual analytical thinking in their hands.

That last part is the most important bit; the most critical problem when considering external normalisation occurs when students substitute AI's organisation of information for their own reasoning process.

When external normalisation becomes AI organising information for you, or even going as far as looking like it has started the analysis process—for example identifying patterns, relationships, or significance—then students once again miss the cognitive work that builds skills. They might feel like they've done the work when they haven't actually developed the ability to break down and analyse for themselves.

Encouraging Positive External Normalisation

- **Data organisation first, analysis second:** Allow AI to help format and categorise information, but require students to identify patterns and draw conclusions independently
- **Separate evidence from interpretation:** Use AI to extract and organise evidence from texts, then have students analyse significance and relationships
- **Create visual frameworks:** Let students use AI to create comparison charts or tables, but they must populate them with their own analytical observations
- **Require analytical justification:** When AI organises information, students must explain why the organisational structure reveals important insights

Analysing & Intentional Offloading

This involves students using AI to create supports that help them remember analytical frameworks, criteria, or systematic approaches to breaking down complex information.

When students ask AI to create rubrics or evaluation criteria for specific problems, they're once again setting up ways where they can remember a process without having to hold it in their mind.

Using AI to create checklists of analytical steps or considerations before completing a task are both examples of intentional offloading as they work as external reminders of the thinking processes needed for thorough analysis.

However as with any other form of intentional offloading with AI, you need to think about scaffolding so students can eventually do these skills independently, without the help of AI to structure these frameworks. When students rely heavily on AI-generated analytical frameworks and checklists without internalising the thinking processes they need to create said frameworks, they may become dependent on external structures that limit their analytical flexibility. The cognitive effort involved in recognising when analysis is needed, selecting appropriate analytical approaches, and developing original interpretations is crucial for building critical thinking expertise. AI that eliminates this effort can actually impede analytical development.

Supporting Strategic Intentional Offloading

- **Build analytical independence gradually:** Start with AI-generated analytical frameworks, progress to student-modified versions, end with student-created frameworks
- **Create 'framework libraries':** Help students build collections of analytical approaches they've internalised, not just AI-generated templates
- **Practice framework selection:** Teach students to choose appropriate analytical approaches for different types of problems without AI guidance

Analysing & Transactive Memory Systems

Where this becomes problematic is when students consistently rely on AI to identify biases, evaluate evidence, or spot logical fallacies rather than developing their own critical reasoning abilities. While AI can provide useful analytical prompts, students who immediately turn to AI for analytical insights miss the opportunity to develop independent critical thinking skills.

This creates a dependency where students cannot engage in sophisticated analysis without external guidance, undermining their ability to think critically in contexts where AI support isn't available.

On the other hand, positive examples of transactive transactive memory systems with AI are therefore found in situations where where AI provides analytical tools, alternative perspectives, or verification support while students maintain ownership of the reasoning and interpretation work. For example, students might use AI to explore counterarguments or alternative interpretations after developing their own analytical conclusions, which represents transactive memory systems because they're leveraging AI's ability to generate different perspectives while maintaining their own critical reasoning. As an added bonus, this is also a good time to ask AI to identify logical fallacies or weak evidence in any arguments they're analysing—including their own!

Preventing Problematic Transactive Memory Systems

- **Develop analytical voice:** Help students recognise and articulate their own interpretive perspectives, not just AI-generated insights
- **Practice bias detection independently:** Regular exercises where students identify assumptions, biases, and logical fallacies without AI assistance
- **Cross-check with multiple sources:** When students use AI for verification, they must also consult human experts and authoritative sources
- **Model humility:** Show how expert analysts—yes, that includes you!—revise their thinking and acknowledge limitations in their interpretations

Thinking Routine #4
The Two-Column Analysis

Side-by-side examination of observations with AI support, done in the vein of a classic See-Think–Wonder routine. Students create three columns with the following headings:

What I see | What this might mean | What else I wonder

They fill the left-hand column entirely with their observations first. Then they work through the middle column, asking AI questions like:

- *What are some possible interpretations of [specific observation]?*
- *Help me think through what [pattern I noticed] might suggest*

Finally, they deepen their thinking more by listing other questions or wonderings that the AI conversation has raised.

Through this activity, students make all the analytical connections, AI provides additional possibilities to consider, and then students continue to take the AI possibilities even further.

Evaluating

***Evaluating* Verbs:** appraise, argue, assess, attach, choose, compare, conclude, contrast, critique, decide, defend, estimate, evaluate, judge, justify, measure, predict, prioritise, prove, rank, rate, recommend, relate, revise, score, select, support, test, validate.

Prompting AI for *Evaluating*: help me evaluate, assess the quality of, critique this approach, judge the effectiveness of, rate the importance of, rank these options by, compare the merits of, contrast the strengths and weaknesses of, decide between alternatives, recommend the best choice from, justify your selection of, defend this position using, argue for or against, measure the success of, prioritise these factors by, score these options based on, choose the most appropriate, conclude whether, estimate the impact of, predict the outcomes of, support my judgement with.

Evaluating & External Normalisation

When students use external normalisation to support with evaluation, what they're really doing is changing how information is presented so that they can make judgements in a more systematic and thorough way.

For example, students might ask AI to organise evaluation criteria into structured rubrics or comparison matrices, making the process of judgement more manageable. Similarly, asking AI to present multiple sources or perspectives side-by-side for comparison represents external normalisation because it organises complex evaluative information into formats that support more rigorous assessment, whilst simultaneously removing some of the cognitive load (and time pressure!) that doing it manually might have taken.

Students might ask AI to create visual representations highlighting strengths and weaknesses of different options, or to format arguments and counter-arguments in structured ways that make weighing evidence more systematic. These approaches reshape the information environment to support more thorough evaluation processes while keeping the actual judgement-making in students' hands.

However, the problem occurs when external normalisation becomes the AI *itself* doing the evaluation rather than the students, meaning they accidentally move from simple restructuring of information to full on AI evaluation of information.

Encouraging Positive External Normalisation

- **Organise evidence, not judgements:** Allow AI to structure comparison charts or format arguments, but require students to make all evaluative decisions independently
- **Create criteria frameworks together:** Use AI to help format evaluation rubrics, but students must determine what criteria matter and why
- **Require justification for all judgements:** When AI organises evaluative information, students must explain their reasoning for every evaluative decision made

Evaluating & Intentional Offloading

At the risk of sounding like a stuck record, here again with intentional offloading what we're looking at is ways that students can create supports to help them think, this time in particular to help them evaluate—that means any kind of evaluative frameworks, criteria, or systematic approaches that will help them to make judgements.

Students might ask AI to generate criteria checklists for evaluating different types of sources, arguments, or solutions, or create reminder systems for considering alternative viewpoints or potential biases.

The key here, as always, is scaffolding toward independence. You want students to eventually internalise these evaluative processes rather than remaining dependent on external supports. When students rely heavily on AI-generated evaluation templates and criteria checklists without developing their own flexible judgement-making processes, they may become dependent on external frameworks that don't account for nuance or context. Most importantly, students need to develop the ability to create original evaluative frameworks when existing templates don't fit the complexity of real-world judgement-making situations.

Supporting Strategic Intentional Offloading

- **Teach criteria selection skills:** Help students learn to choose appropriate evaluation standards for different contexts without AI guidance
- **Practice independent criteria development:** Regular exercises where students create evaluation standards without AI assistance
- **Comparative judgement exercises:** Students evaluate the same issue using different criteria to build evaluative flexibility
- **Regular template-free evaluation:** Schedule sessions where students evaluate without any external structural support

Evaluating & Transactive Memory Systems

At this point in their learning journey, students can develop a thought partnership with AI where they maintain ownership of judgement-making while leveraging AI's capabilities to strengthen and test their evaluation skills.

After developing their own initial assessment framework, students might ask AI to suggest additional evaluation criteria they hadn't considered, using AI as a brainstorming partner rather than a decision-maker. They could also use AI to test the strength of their arguments or identify potential weaknesses in their reasoning after forming their own judgements, essentially using AI as a devil's advocate to refine their thinking. They could ask AI to provide examples of how others have evaluated similar issues differently, expanding their understanding of evaluative possibilities while maintaining their own reasoned conclusions.

The goal is developing expertise in knowing when to seek AI input for additional evidence or alternative viewpoints versus when to trust their own evaluative reasoning and values.

The danger emerges when this becomes a crutch rather than a tool. Students who consistently seek AI validation for their evaluation criteria, evidence-weighing, or final judgements risk never developing confidence in their own evaluative reasoning abilities. This dependency is particularly problematic because it's rooted in their own values and experiences—something AI cannot and should not replace, particularly when we remember its WEIRD bias. When students can't make evaluative decisions without external confirmation, they lose the ability to engage authentically with complex issues requiring personal judgement. The productive struggle of wrestling with competing values, incomplete information, and conflicting criteria is exactly what builds sophisticated evaluative thinking that can adapt to novel situations and reflect genuine personal reasoning.

Preventing Problematic Transactive Memory Systems

- **Require judgement-first protocols:** Students must complete their own evaluative reasoning before consulting AI for additional perspectives

- **Connect evaluation to personal identity:** Help students understand how their evaluative abilities reflect their values and reasoning
- **Evaluative dialogue assessments:** Test students' ability to defend and refine their judgements through discussion without AI support

Thinking Routine #5
The Iceberg Assessment

This thinking routine allows students to consider both the visible and hidden aspects of a situation they are evaluating. You may wish to get them to draw an iceberg to fully grasp the idea of visible versus hidden.

Above water (Obviously visible aspects):

- What can everyone see about quality/value here?
- What's the immediate, surface-level evaluation?

Below water (Hidden implications and consequences):

- What deeper effects or qualities might not be immediately apparent?
- How do hidden factors change the overall evaluation?

Students can give their considerations to an AI tool and ask it to point out or question less obvious implications, but students judge the significance of AI-generated information for overall evaluation.

Thinking Routine #6
The Two-Column Truth Test

A bonus one, because why not! A simple side-by-side evaluation where students make a table with two columns:

Evidence for | Evidence against

Students fill both columns completely before making judgements, then ask AI: "What evidence might I be missing in either column?"

They then look at both columns together and consider which side is more convincing and why.

Creating

***Creating* Verbs:** assemble, build, combine, compile, compose, construct, create, design, develop, devise, formulate, generate, hypothesise, invent, make, organise, originate, plan, prepare, produce, propose, set up, synthesise, write.

Prompting AI for *Creating*: help me create, generate ideas for, brainstorm options to, design a new, develop a plan for, build upon this concept to, construct a framework for, compose a piece that, write a draft of, synthesise these elements into, combine these ideas to form, assemble components for, compile information into, formulate a strategy to, devise a solution that, invent a new approach to, propose a method for, hypothesise about, produce an example of, plan the steps to create, set up a system for, organise materials to build.

Creating & External Normalisation

When students ask AI to help format their original writing into proper manuscript structure or create visual layouts for their creative projects, they're not so much offloading the creative work as making it easier to do the creative work that *matters*. They can offload the cognitive work of arranging ideas, and put more thought into the ideas themselves. Think of this as AI handling the wrapping while students create the actual gift! AI can organise and structure the presentation of creative work, but the creative thinking, original ideas, and innovative solutions must come entirely from students.

This type of support can actually enhance creativity by removing administrative burdens and allowing students to focus their cognitive energy on the creative work itself. On the other hand, the negative side of external normalisation happens when students get AI creating original writing, visual designs, or conceptual frameworks, producing impressive-looking work without developing independent capability to generate, develop, and refine original ideas.

Encouraging Positive External Normalisation

- **Separate technical from creative:** AI can handle formatting and organisation, students handle all creative thinking
- **Monitor for content substitution:** Watch for students who let AI influence their actual creative ideas
- **Reality-check original thinking:** Regular verification that creative work genuinely reflects student thinking

Creating & Intentional Offloading

At this level, intentional offloading can be helpful for helping students remember creative strategies, maintain project momentum, or systematically approach creative challenges.

Students can stimulate their own creative thinking without AI generating actual ideas by getting the AI to brainstorm prompts or creative exercises for future use—this becomes a way to offload the process as they no longer need to think about these creative exercises, they can simply get going with the act of creation.

This said, when students rely on AI-generated creative frameworks and idea prompts without struggling through the productive confusion of creative work, they can become dependent on external creative stimulation rather than developing internal creative resources. In other words, if they don't struggle through creative blocks and develop their own personal creative processes, then they may struggle to build genuine creative capacity.

They may produce impressive-looking work with the support of AI, but they haven't developed the independent capability to generate, develop, and refine original ideas, which is the entire point of creative assignments. The moment AI starts contributing creative content rather than just organising it, students lose the authentic creative experience that builds their innovative thinking abilities.

Supporting Strategic Intentional Offloading

- **Build creative independence gradually:** Start with AI-generated prompts, progress to student-created exercises, end with independent creative processes
- **Regular prompt-free creativity:** Schedule sessions where students create without any external creative supports
- **Build creative habits:** Students develop daily creative practices that don't rely on external prompts

Creating & Transactive Memory Systems

Here, students develop partnerships where AI provides technical support, alternative perspectives, or creative feedback while the student maintains ownership of actually coming up with the idea and making creative decisions.

After developing initial drafts or prototypes, students might ask AI for feedback on their creative work, using AI as a partner for refining their original ideas. They could use AI to explore technical aspects like research support or factual verification while maintaining creative control over conceptual development, or ask AI to suggest alternative approaches after developing their own developing creativity.

The danger emerges when students consistently rely on AI to generate ideas, solve creative problems, or make creative decisions rather than developing their own innovative thinking abilities. This creates dependency where students cannot engage in authentic creative work without external idea generation, fundamentally undermining the purpose of creative education.

Most concerning is when AI prevents students from experiencing the full creative cycle, struggling with ambiguity, persisting through iterations, learning from creative failures, and developing personal standards for creative quality—the true fun of the creative journey!

Preventing Problematic Transactive Memory Systems

- **Require creation-first protocols:** Students must complete substantial original creative work before seeking any AI input
- **Separate technical from creative feedback:** AI can help with technical aspects, but creative decisions must remain with students. This goes for the feedback you give them as well—consider separating your feedback to refer to both parts separately.
- **Foster authentic creative identity:** Help students discover and develop their unique creative capabilities and interests
- **Create feedback communities:** Encourage peer collaboration and feedback before turning to AI input
- **Cultivate creative patience:** Help students understand that meaningful creative work takes time and sustained effort

Thinking Routine #7
The Original Vision Framework

Protecting creative ownership while using AI support through using this step by step thinking routine: VISION - VOICE - CRAFT - REFLECT

VISION: Establish your creative direction

- What unique idea, perspective, or solution do I want to create?
- What personal experience, insight, or passion drives this creative work?
- What would make this genuinely mine rather than generic?
- How does my individual perspective shape what I want to create?

VOICE: Develop your distinctive approach

- What's my unique way of expressing or developing this idea?
- How do my values, experiences, and interests influence my creative choices?
- What creative decisions reflect my personal style or thinking?
- Where do I want to take creative risks or try something new?

CRAFT: Build with strategic AI partnership

- Where can AI help with technical skills while I maintain creative control?
- Ask AI: *Can you help me research [technical aspect] without suggesting creative content?*
- Use AI for organisation, formatting, or procedural support: *Help me structure my creative work according to [format] while keeping my content unchanged*
- How can AI support my creative process without replacing my creative thinking?

REFLECT: Validate creative authenticity

- Can I explain every creative choice I made and why I made it?
- What parts of this work genuinely represent my own thinking and creativity?
- How has my creative capacity actually grown through this process?
- Would I be able to create similar original work independently in the future?

Metacognition

6

The Metacognitive Cycle

A few years ago, I was introduced to Professors Bill Cope and Mary Kalantzis' work on the seven digital affordances—the idea that when you're using digital technologies in the classroom, they have certain affordances or things that they provide students that they wouldn't otherwise be able to do. It's a great framework to help you consider the purpose of any technologies that you bring into the classroom. If you've not come across the affordances before, they are (in no particular order):

- Ubiquitous learning
- Active knowledge making
- Multimodal meaning
- Recursive feedback
- Differentiated learning
- Collaborative intelligence
- And... metacognition.

Over the years, I would run professional learning sessions linked to the digital affordances, and every year we would focus on a different affordance or two so that we could really dig in to how we were providing support in digital learning for both students and teachers.

So here I was, running some pretty high quality training (if I do say so myself), when leadership decided that our next focus should be metacognition.

And now I have an admission to make.

You see, I'd read the books. Watched the videos. Knew [some of] the research. And when everyone kept saying, "Metacognition is just thinking about thinking!" there I was, nodding along, saying, "sure, totally!" Because, well, it made sense!

Sort of.

My initial understanding of metacognition was exactly what they were saying: that it is thinking about thinking and understanding how I (and my students) learn best. But repeating the mantra is one thing. Actually knowing what it looks like in practice—and what it means for your students!—is a whole other kettle of fish.

* * *

The Education Endowment Foundation has what I think is one of the clearest definitions of metacognition. They describe it as a cyclical process isn't just 'thinking about thinking', but actually understanding your own learning process. The cycle has three parts, each just as important as the others, and each feeding into the next.

Planning is the first part of the cycle. This is when you prepare for learning or work out how you're going to tackle something. It's the moment when you ask yourself: *What don't I know yet? What do I need to know? Which strategies are going to give me the best chance of success?* It's about making a plan, rather than just diving in and hoping for the best.

Then comes **monitoring**—that's checking in on your learning while it's actually happening. This might be a formal pause or a continuous self-check that happens in the background, but the point is that you need to know what's going on in your learning as it unfolds.

Story time!

In my first year of teaching, my NQT mentor taught me about the importance of 'pit stops' in lessons. In the Languages Department, the rule was that you had to have at least two pit stops per lesson, so that your overall lesson outline was something along the lines of: *Starter, Activity, Pit Stop 1, Activity, Pit Stop 2, Activity, Plenary.* A pit stop could be a quick set of questions, a short game, or a mini task that took five minutes or less. So for example if I was teaching the French past tense, the *passé composé*, I might pause the lesson, have students quickly conjugate their verbs on mini whiteboards, and in a few minutes I could tell whether they'd understood the concept or not, and who might need a bit more guidance or further extension.

The thing is, those pit stops were really about *my* monitoring of *their* learning. I was checking where they were at, but they weren't learning to check for themselves. That's actually a really handy way of understanding the difference between what we might traditionally call assessment for learning versus what I'm talking about here; the 'monitoring' element of metacognition.

The final stage before we loop back around the cycle is **evaluating**, where students reflect on their learning journey. This might happen at the end of a lesson, a unit, a day, or any natural stopping point, and it's when they ask: *What did I learn? What* didn't *I learn? What went well? What will I change next time?* And because it's a cycle, that evaluation naturally feeds into planning for the next piece of learning, which then leads to monitoring, then back to evaluating again.

Of course, it's never quite as straightforward as that! Research suggests that many students don't naturally have the skills to monitor their own learning effectively. They might not know how to evaluate their learning. And of course, anyone who has tried to wrangle a group of young students through any sort of extended project all know that you need to teach planning rather than assume it comes naturally.

Overall, this just means that metacognition something we need to teach explicitly—and if we're going to plan how to do that, we might as well think about how we teach it with AI too.

But wait, there's more!

I actually want to take us one step further than just 'plan, monitor, evaluate' by looking at Roger Azevedo's work on enhancing metacognitive adaptivity and personalisation. His views of the metacognitive cycle are similar to those of the EEF, but he breaks them down a little further as:

- **Judgements of learning,** where students decide how well they think they've learned something
- **Feelings of knowing**, where they sense whether a piece of information is accessible from memory
- **Content evaluation**, where they judge the quality and relevance of information
- **Monitoring** progress towards goals
- **Monitoring** whether chosen strategies are working
- **Self-questioning** to test and deepen understanding

Looking at metacognition through this lens further develops how we approach it in the classroom. As well as thinking of the cycle as those three main steps, we can also break it down into a network of self-awareness behaviours, each of which can be taught, practised, and strengthened over time. The more specific we are about what these processes look like in action, the easier it becomes to design activities that help students take ownership of them.

This is also where AI starts to make things interesting... and maybe more complicated.

You see, in a classroom where metacognition is actively taught and modeled, students will see each element of the cycle in action. They'll watch a teacher work through a maths problem, narrating the decisions being made along the way. They hear a classmate explain how they approached planning an essay. Throughout all of this, they're exposed to a thinking *path*, not just the finished product. Those visible moments are where metacognitive skills can take root, because students can see what monitoring, evaluating, and adjusting actually look like.

With AI, that path is often hidden.

Students type in a question, and what they see is the polished answer. The planning, the choices, the false starts—all of that is invisible. Even with reasoning models that ostensibly 'show their working' or outline their 'thought processes', you're still not seeing genuine thinking. Don't get me wrong; these can be a good facsimile of what thinking looks like, and I've shared many times that it's a great way to get students to understand what 'show your thinking' could look like, but it's still not human reasoning, and it doesn't necessarily help a student practise their own metacognitive thinking. In fact, if you're not careful it can encourage them to focus more on interpreting the AI's process than on developing their own.

There's also the risk students developing a level of metacognitive co-dependency. When AI can handle parts of the planning, monitoring, and evaluation for them, it's all too easy for them to just... *let it.*

Just like over-relying on GPS can make us less confident in finding our own way around, over-relying on AI can weaken the mental muscles we use for self-awareness and self-regulation. This is particularly true for younger learners, who might see AI use as an all-or-nothing choice—either the AI does the whole thing, or they do. But real growth in metacognitive skill happens in the messy middle, where the student still has to make decisions, try strategies, check progress, and adjust course as they go.

That's why, when we talk about teaching metacognition with AI in the mix, we also need to consider self-regulated learning as yet another ingredient in our every-developing thought smoothie. Self-regulated learning is about being aware of yourself, managing yourself, and taking control of your own learning—whether that's choosing the right strategy, setting up your environment, or handling the emotions that affect how you work.

The clue is in the name: *self*-regulated. Not AI-regulated, not teacher-regulated, and certainly not left entirely to a machine.

When I look back at my early 'pit stop' lessons, I realise that's exactly what I was missing. The monitoring was happening, but I was doing it to students rather than supporting them to do it for themselves. In those moments, they weren't learning to recognise what was working or what wasn't, and they certainly weren't learning how to make adjustments in response. There was neither self-regulation nor self-monitoring. There was just... teacher.

For monitoring to be truly metacognitive, students need to be the ones checking in, identifying where they're making progress, spotting the gaps, and deciding how to address them. And that doesn't just apply to monitoring—it's the same for planning and evaluating too. To engage in any of these stages effectively, they first need to understand how they learn, what strategies are available to them, and how to recognise when they don't know something.

And then there's the hurdle that we teachers all know a bit too well: time.

There's this idea that metacognition is something huge and extra, something you need to take specific time out of your lesson to 'achieve' in an already busy programme of learning. But here's the thing: you're probably already doing it, even if you don't realise it yet.

You may not recognise this one unless you've explicitly taught in a British classroom, but Nando's-themed choice boards have long been (and, I think, continue to be) the absolute pinnacle of classroom displays in schools across the United Kingdom.

For those of you who haven't had the joy of a cheeky Nando's, it's a popular chicken restaurant chain where part of the 'experience' is allowing you to choose how spicy you want your chicken from mild to varying levels of hot. It doesn't matter whether we're talking chicken goujons, chicken burgers, or even an entire chicken on a plate, you can use the heat scale to customise your order to your liking.

In the classroom, this heat scale translates to activity choice boards where students are given the option to select an activity ranging from 'mild'—usually the less challenging or complicated task—through to various versions of 'hot', replete with multiple chilli icons and activities that get more challenging (or from time to time, more convoluted!) the hotter you go. It might be a bit of a dated example and I'm not sure how popular it is in today's classroom, but it's a great way to explain that you're probably already practicing elements of the metacognitive cycle with your students, even if you don't realise it yet.

You see, if you've ever used something like a Nando's scale to let students choose the level of challenge for a task, you've been supporting the planning stage of the metacognitive cycle. The trick for developing it further? If you follow that up by asking why they chose, say, 'medium' instead of 'extra hot', you're now nudging them into deeper metacognitive territory by getting them to articulate the reasoning behind their choice.

Or to go for a simpler, non-chicken example, if you've used exit tickets where students jot down what they learned and what challenged them, you've been prompting the evaluation stage. Learning logs, think–pair–share with a reflection step, self-assessment rubrics—all of these are ways of making the learning process more visible to the learner. And they're all things teachers have done at least once in their time in the classroom! In other words, I don't want you to panic as you look at this chapter and realise that this is just another thing you have to add to an already busy lesson plan. You're doing it already.

And so finally we get to the AI of it all.

Back in the critical thinking section, we talked about the difference between thinking alongside AI and letting AI do the thinking for you—the centaur and cyborg approaches—and the importance of being intentional about which mode we choose. Now we're looking at that metacognitive cycle: planning, monitoring, and evaluating, with Azevedo's slightly more complex elements threaded through. Again, it's about being intentional at every step.

Both sets of theory form the foundation for what we're looking at in this section, because metacognition and critical thinking are closely linked; you can't do one well without the other.

Think about Daniel Willingham's three elements of critical thinking—novelty, self-direction, and effectiveness—and you can further see how they map neatly onto the metacognitive cycle. Novelty and self-direction show up when students are planning their approach; effectiveness comes into play when they monitor and evaluate how well it's working. The skills we've already discussed are not separate boxes to tick but parts of a much bigger, connected picture of how students think, learn, and make decisions.

That means that, at least to a certain extent, you probably already have a firm foundation in how AI might support with metacognition, even if you don't realise it yet.

* * *

Research shows that students get better at using metacognitive strategies—the learning logs, the reflection journals, the choice boards—when they not only know what the strategies are, but also when and how to use them effectively. It's at this point where AI becomes both a potential aid and a potential obstacle. The same tools that can help students plan, monitor, and evaluate more efficiently can also tempt them to skip those steps entirely. Our job is therefore to design opportunities where they still have to do the thinking, even when AI is part of the process, so they leave the classroom stronger in their metacognitive skills, not weaker.

Before we get too excited, here's an important caveat: I can't point you to a neat stack of studies that prove AI improves metacognitive outcomes. As far as I can tell, those studies don't yet exist. We're still too early in the game.

But I'd argue that it's a bit like Richard E. Clark's argument back in 1983 that different forms of media are like different types of truck delivering groceries—it doesn't matter what kind of truck turns up, the nutritional value of the groceries is the same. It doesn't matter how (by way of TV, books, or podcasts) I learn information (the groceries) so long as I learn it! You could apply that logic here: maybe it's not the truck (AI) that matters, but the groceries (metacognitive processes) themselves. The value is in doing the metacognition, not in whether AI was involved.

So why bring AI into it at all? Because it might help scaffold those processes. It might support students who struggle with traditional approaches, or give a voice to those who are too shy to reflect openly with teachers or peers. It might make metacognition more accessible, more personal, and, for some students, more engaging. Even if the 'nutritional value' doesn't change, the delivery method might mean more students actually get fed.

There's also something unique about the dialogue AI enables. Reflection doesn't have to be a lonely one-way street written in a journal. With AI, students can talk about their thinking in real time, and the back-and-forth might push them to think more deeply than a tick-box reflection ever could. It could help them focus on what they've actually learned, rather than just going through the motions. And let's face it: the ability to have a productive, reflective conversation with an AI tool is a skill that might be just as valuable in the workplace as it is in school.

The challenge for us is to make sure AI is used as a thinking partner, not just an answer machine. That means building structured opportunities for students to engage with it in ways that strengthen their planning, monitoring, and evaluating, whilst scaffolding both their metacognitive skills and their ability to get the best out of AI.

7

Thinking Aloud

It's pretty likely that at some point in your life—whether in the classroom or outside of it—you've come across the concept of the 'think-aloud'. It's that process where someone (usually an expert) models their thinking process out loud for others to study and learn from. Think-alouds have been around for decades: a teacher solving a maths problem while verbalising their thought process, a reading specialist demonstrating how they make predictions about a text. They're simple but powerful! By making thinking audible, we make it visible, accessible, and ultimately, learnable. And as AI becomes an increasingly significant part of our educational landscape, applying this classic teaching technique to AI interactions is the next logical step for developing genuine metacognition around AI usage.

If you've already encountered think-alouds in a pedagogical sense, it's highly likely to have been in the context of reading instruction. That's certainly where most journal articles seem to base their research. The reading teacher reads a passage aloud to the class and says something like, "Hmm, this character seems anxious. I can tell because the author mentioned their 'trembling hands' and 'darting eyes'. I'm going to predict that something stressful is about to happen..." They're modelling their thinking to their students.

But limiting think-alouds to reading instruction misses their broader potential. The EEF research highlights how they're valuable across the *entire* curriculum. Whether it's a science teacher walking through experimental design decisions, a PE teacher articulating tactical thinking in sports, or a music teacher verbalising their interpretive choices while performing, the metacognitive benefits extend far beyond reading comprehension.

What makes think-alouds so powerful is their versatility. They work effectively across diverse subjects because metacognitive processes are universal, though they manifest differently in each discipline. This universality makes think-alouds a tool that can be consistently reinforced across a student's entire school experience.

But why do they work?

Well, it's because they externalise the internal (I know, fancy!). They transform abstract cognitive processes into concrete, observable behaviours that students can notice, name, and eventually adopt for their own learning. When a teacher models their thinking, they're essentially providing a kind of cognitive apprenticeship—letting students observe an expert's thought patterns before trying out similar strategies themselves.

And then there's the real magic, which happens when think-alouds make visible not just the *what* but the *why* behind decisions. It's the difference between "I'm going to reread this paragraph" and "I'm going to reread this paragraph *because* I noticed I'm confused about the author's main point, and confusion is usually a signal that I need to slow down and check my understanding."

As I mentioned in the previous chapter, explicitly teaching metacognitive strategies significantly impacts both students' metacognitive development and their overall achievement. And guess what? Think-alouds are tailor-made for precisely this purpose. Even better, if we want our students to think more strategically about their use of AI, think-alouds offer a perfect solution.

To really make sure we're going as deep as we can for this part, I want to combine the EEF work with Azevedo's. That means you'll likely see a bit of repetition in these next few explanations (but hopefully not in the example AI prompts themselves!) as Azevedo's work weaves in and out. That's okay! Metacognition isn't a perfect circle. It's more of a ball of wibbly wobbly, metacognition-y... stuff.

What I'm trying to say it that, as always, take your pick of what works and what doesn't. Test them with yourself in the comfort of your own office-classroom-house-garden-wherever and see how you feel. If you have one to hand, I can recommend also testing them on a cat. They make an excellent, non-judgmental audience.

Mostly, anyway.

* * *

The Planning Phase

Feelings of knowing

Students plan by working out what they already know and where they need to go next. This helps them decide how much AI support they actually need and what specific areas to focus on.

- Before I type this prompt, let me think a little first. I know ... but I'm unclear about ...

- I should tell the AI that I already understand ... so it doesn't repeat that information
- I'm going to mention in my prompt that I'm confused about ... specifically
- Let me start my prompt by explaining what I already know: ...
- Before I ask the AI anything, let me think about what I already understand about ...
- I'm pretty confident about ... but I'm completely lost when it comes to ...
- I have a feeling I learned about ... before, but I should ask the AI to refresh my memory on ...

Monitoring progress towards goals

Students think about what they are actually trying to do with the AI. Setting clear objectives upfront helps them to stay focused and recognise when they've achieved what they set out to do.

- I'm going to type a prompt that focuses on ... because that's what I need so I can ...
- Let me make sure my question asks for ... since that's my main goal
- I should mention in my prompt that I'm trying to ... so the AI gives me relevant help
- I'm going to be specific and ask for ... rather than a general explanation
- I want to accomplish ... today, which means I should focus my AI questions on ...
- By the end of this, I need to be able to ... so let me ask the AI for ...

- I'm trying to learn ..., so I should ask the AI to ...

The Monitoring Phase

Content evaluation

At this stage, it's time for students to ask: *Is this AI response accurate, relevant, and helpful for my purpose?* Real-time quality checking prevents them from building new understanding on faulty information.

- As I'm reading this response, ... sounds right but ... seems questionable
- This part about ... matches what I know, but this claim about ... needs checking
- The AI is giving me good information about ... but it's not talking about ...
- It looks the AI assumed ... but I actually meant ...
- The AI seems accurate because ... but I should double-check ...
- The AI just told me ... which contradicts what I thought about ...
- This explanation from the AI makes sense for ... but doesn't address my question about ...
- I need to verify what the AI said about ... because ...

Monitoring strategy effectiveness

Checking whether their methods are effective lets students adjust their approach before wasting more time chatting pointlessly to the AI; in a nutshell, they ask: *is what I'm doing with AI actually working?*

- This response shows me that my prompt was too focused on... so I need to adjust it to ...
- The AI understood the ... part of my question but missed the ... part
- I'm getting a generic answer, so let me try asking for ... instead
- This isn't what I wanted, let me rephrase and ask specifically about ...
- My prompt worked well because the AI gave me ... but next time I should ask for ...
- The AI isn't understanding what I want, so let me try rephrasing my question to focus on ...
- This approach of asking the AI to ... is working better than when I asked it to ...
- I'm not getting useful responses, so I should change my strategy to ...

Self-questioning

Getting students to take their thinking beyond surface level answers is a difficult, but rewarding, part of the metacognition journey. It helps them develop genuine understanding rather than just collecting information to use (or not use!) later.

- While reading this, I'm wondering, what about ...?
- This makes me think about ... maybe I'll ask a follow-up about that
- If this is true, then maybe ... is also true. I should check that.
- I'm going to ask the AI to explain why ... happens because I don't understand that part
- This makes me think, what would happen if ... instead of ...?

- I understand what the AI said about ... but how does that connect to ...?
- The AI answer raises a new question for me: why does ... happen when ...?

Monitoring progress towards goals

The overall question here is simple: Am I getting closer to my learning target, or am I going off track? Regular progress checks help students stay focused on their learning and recognise when they need to redirect their efforts.

- This output is helping me with ... but I still need information about ...
- I'm getting what I need for ... but let me also ask about ... while I'm here
- This is useful but I need to ask a more specific question about ... to get to where I want to go
- It feels like I'm getting closer to understanding ... but I still need to figure out ...
- I need to refocus my AI questions on ... because that's what will help me understand ... better

The Evaluating Phase

Judgements of learning

Honest self-assessment of their learning helps students identify what they've truly mastered versus what they've just been exposed to through chatting with the AI, ready to plan their next steps.

- Now that I've read all these responses, I feel solid on ... but shaky on ...
- Let me ask the AI to quiz me on ... to see if I really understand it
- I think I get it, but let me try explaining ... back to the AI to test myself
- Before I finish, let me ask the AI one clarifying question about ...
- After working with AI this time, I feel confident about ... but I still need practice with ...
- If someone asked me about this topic now, I could explain ... but I'd struggle with ...

Content evaluation

At this point in the learning journey, metacognition becomes about looking back to how reliable and useful the information was that the AI came up with. Final quality assessment helps students decide how much to trust and use what they've learned.

- Looking back at this conversation, the AI was most helpful when it explained ...

- I should double-check what the AI said about ... with another source
- The AI gave me a good overview but I notice it didn't mention ... at all
- Overall this was useful for ... but I need to look elsewhere for ...
- The AI's response was biased toward ... so I should also research ...

Evaluating strategy effectiveness

As they wrap up this phase, it's worth building in time for students to see which techniques worked and which didn't. This helps them become more strategic and effective in their future AI use.

- I got better responses when I asked for ... rather than ...
- Next time I should start with some more context about ... to get more targeted help
- The most useful prompt I used was when I asked the AI to ...
- I wasted time when I ... so I won't do that again
- The most effective way I used AI today was ... and I should do more of that!
- I learned that the AI responds better when I ... compared to when I ...
- My biggest mistake was ... and next time I'll approach it by ...

The Science of Learning

8

What is Learning, Really?

Already in this book we've explored a couple of big ideas: how to think critically with AI, how to be aware of your own cognitive processes (and whether or not you're offloading them) and how to become metacognitive—to notice, plan, monitor, and evaluate your own learning. Now it's time to add another essential layer. This section introduces more about the science of learning, moving on from elements we've already looked at like metacognition and cognitive load, and going deeper into more evidence-based principles from cognitive psychology, neuroscience, and education that explain how we actually acquire, process, and retain knowledge. These aren't educational trends or quick tips, but robust findings from decades of research about what makes learning effective and durable.

If metacognition is about being aware of yourself as a learner and actively steering your own process, these additional science of learning strategies are about understanding the cognitive mechanisms that underlie that process. Think of it this way: metacognition gives you the ability to monitor and adjust your approach, whilst the science of learning reveals why certain approaches work and others don't. It's the difference between knowing that retrieval practice helps you remember things, and understanding that it works because it strengthens neural pathways through effortful recall.

This understanding becomes particularly crucial when we introduce AI into educational contexts. AI can make certain aspects of learning more efficient, but it can also inadvertently bypass the processes that make learning stick. Without understanding the underlying principles, we can't distinguish between genuine support and problematic shortcuts.

Over the coming chapters, we're going explore these key principles in detail. You might notice that I'm not covering every single element of learning science here—for example, we don't talk about metacognition or cognitive load... but in my defence, that's because we've already done it in detail! Think of this section of the book as a quick flyover of the 'other' parts of learning science. And who knows, maybe another book will come out of them one of these days...

* * *

Retrieval Practice and the Testing Effect

Research shows us that actively retrieving information from memory strengthens learning far more than re-reading or reviewing notes. This 'testing effect' shows that the effort of recall itself changes how memories are stored and accessed.

The key here is the effort. When we struggle to remember something and then successfully retrieve it, we strengthen those neural pathways. Relying on Apple Maps to get around a new town means you're going to be slower to learn your way around rather than if you just get lost a few times and try to remember the way yourself; when you force yourself to remember that 'tip of the tongue' fact rather than looking it up straight away, it'll come easier next time.

That, unfortunately, is the issue with AI. It makes information—whether it's true *or* false!—instantly available, removing that need for effortful recall. A student who immediately asks an AI tool to give them the key points about a topic they studied yesterday misses the opportunity to strengthen that memory through retrieval. That said, there's still scope for AI to support in retrieval practice if it's used as a tool to help you retrieve, rather than doing the retrieving for you. As you'll see throughout this chapter (and, to be honest, you've been seeing throughout this book!), it's all about how it's done.

Spaced versus Massed Practice

Cramming might feel productive (go back to my example of writing out vocabulary on repeat for hours for a great example of that productivity illusion!), but decades of research show that spacing out practice over time leads to much better long-term retention. This 'spacing effect', first documented by Ebbinghaus in the 1880s and refined by countless studies since, shows that we remember things better when we review them at increasing intervals.

The thing is that spaced practice feels harder and less immediately rewarding than massed practice. Students often feel like they're learning more when they study everything at once, even though the opposite is true for long-term retention.

AI could be brilliant at implementing spacing—supporting in the creation of a revision calendar, generating practice problems on the right topics, or tracking what needs revision based on unit outlines. But it could also enable the worst kind of cramming if students use it to quickly generate summaries of everything the night before an exam.

The tool itself is neutral; the understanding of spacing principles determines whether it helps or hinders.

Productive Struggle and Desirable Difficulties

This one might seem counterintuitive in our efficiency-obsessed age, but certain types of difficulty actually improve learning. This is linked to what I said a moment ago about retrieval practice requiring effort: Robert Bjork's concept of 'desirable difficulties' shows that when we have to work harder to learn something we often learn it better.

These difficulties might include having to generate your own answers rather than recognising them (i.e. writing a short sentence rather than circling the correct one), interleaving different types of problems rather than blocking them together, or having to elaborate on concepts in your own words. As always, the struggle itself is part of what makes learning stick.

AI's efficiency can be the enemy of productive struggle. If a student asks AI to explain something they're confused about, and it immediately provides a perfect explanation, that might feel helpful but actually short-circuit the thinking process that leads to deep understanding. Again you should start to see connections to other things we've talked about throughout the book, where engaging your brain more is going to take you from a passive user of AI to someone who thinks while using it! In a nutshell, effective AI users need to recognise when productive struggle is, well, productive, versus when an AI can provide support to scaffold the learning a little more.

Transfer of Learning and Schema Building

As educators we know that learning isn't just about memorising isolated facts; it's about building organised mental models (schemas) that allow us to apply knowledge in new situations. Teaching students how to transfer—to use what they've learned in one context to solve problems in another—might even be one of the most important things we do!

Schema building requires making connections, seeing patterns, and understanding underlying principles. It's the difference between memorising that 2+2=4 and understanding the actual concept of addition. Strong schemas allow us to chunk information efficiently, recognise patterns quickly, and apply knowledge flexibly.

AI therefore poses interesting questions for transfer and schema building, because on one hand, it can help by making connections visible, showing multiple examples, or explaining underlying patterns. But on the other hand, if students become dependent on AI to make connections for them, they might not develop the schemas that allow independent transfer.

* * *

The next part of the book is going to dig in a little deeper to each of these elements of the science of learning. At the end of each chapter are some actionable uses of AI that you can put into practice with your students. Some are activities, some are sample prompts, all of them are tried and tested ways to develop thinking. You can read linearly, or you can jump between chapters depending on what you need.

9

Take it Back now, Y'all: Retrieval Practice

Here's something I've noticed happening over the past few years: we've started treating memory like it's optional. Forget the capital city of Luxembourg? Pull out your phone and do a quick Google. Come across a tricky word in an old book? No need to try and decode it based on context, you can probably highlight it in the Kindle app or do another quick online search to grab the definition. And forgotten that formula for calculating velocity? Don't worry: AI's got it covered.

But here's the thing we're forgetting (ironic, I know): students still need things in their heads. Not because we're old-fashioned, not because we're resisting progress, but because that's literally how learning works.

You can't analyse a text you can't remember. You can't solve problems without holding multiple concepts in your working memory simultaneously. You can't build understanding from components you have to look up every single time. Knowledge isn't just what you can access; it's what you can think with. And as we should all know by now,

AI can't do the remembering for you—or at least, not in a way that translates into actual, transferable learning.

Retrieval practice is the act of pulling information from memory without looking at notes or resources—like trying to recall the causes of World War I from memory rather than re-reading them, or trying to remember that really good quote to prove your point in an argument.

When Hermann Ebbinghaus mapped out the forgetting curve back in the 1880s, he showed that we lose most new information within days unless we actively work to retain it. Our brains are remarkably efficient at dumping what seems irrelevant. On the plus side, though, each time we retrieve information, we reset and flatten that curve. The memory becomes more durable, more accessible, more permanent.

I mentioned the 'testing effect' in the last chapter. It's the idea that actively retrieving information from memory—or in other words, flattening the curve once more—strengthens learning far more than simply reviewing the information through re-reading, highlighting, or just hoping for the best.

When it comes to techniques that improve retention, retrieval practice consistently outperforms re-reading or passive review across all age groups and subject areas. Another classroom-based study showed that students who incorporated regular retrieval practice retained 40% more content after six weeks compared to those using traditional review methods. Then there's the student responses themselves. Studies have shown that students who rated their confidence after retrieval attempts not only improved their accuracy over time but also developed better metacognitive awareness. They learned to distinguish between what they actually knew and what merely felt familiar.

Here's where AI creates a particular challenge. Students consistently confuse fluency with learning. When information flows smoothly—when an AI instantly provides the perfect explanation, when everything feels easy—students believe they're learning effectively. But they're not. It's the illusion of competency. A student who's just read an AI-generated summary feels like they understand the content. A student who's asked ChatGPT to remind them of key concepts feels prepared for the test. But recognition isn't retrieval, and familiarity isn't knowledge. Or, in other words, we have to actively teach them what retrieval really is, why it's important, and how (or if!) AI can support them.

A quick note on recognition versus retrieval

Let me be crystal clear about this distinction because it matters enormously for how we use AI. Recognition is seeing the right answer and thinking "yes, that's it." Retrieval is producing the answer from memory. They're neurologically different processes, and they lead to fundamentally different learning outcomes.

When a student uses AI to generate multiple choice questions and then selects answers, that's primarily recognition. When they read an AI summary and nod along, that's recognition. Even when they prompt AI for information they've seen before, if the answer appears instantly, that's closer to recognition than retrieval.

So where does this leave us with AI? AI can be brilliant at creating retrieval opportunities. It can generate questions at exactly the right level of difficulty. It can help students to understand how to space practice optimally over time. It can provide immediate, detailed feedback after retrieval attempts. It can adapt to individual students' knowledge gaps and strengths. But—and this is the key part—*only* if we maintain the effort where it belongs: with the student. In the context of retrieval practice, you can think of AI as a sophisticated quiz master, not an answer machine. It can create the questions, help outline the 'when' of the practice, provide the feedback, to a certain extent track the progress. But the student still has to do the actual retrieving. The moment we let AI do the remembering for them, we've lost the plot entirely.

So, here are a few tactics that might support AI-powered retrieval. Unlike other chapters thus far, here I'm going to give you said tactics in context. Just swap your own subject/context for what I've provided, and see how you get on. There are just a few non-negotiable to keep in mind for all of the strategies we look at in order for the strategy to be truly linked to retrieval practice:

- The student must generate the answer from memory, not select or recognise it
- There must be some effort involved—if it's too easy, it's not retrieval
- Feedback should come *after* the retrieval attempt, not during
- Spacing matters more than massing—little and often beats cramming every time

* * *

Retrieval Strategy #1

The Generate-Then-Retrieve Method

Instead of students using AI to quiz themselves directly, have them use it to create retrieval opportunities that they'll complete offline.

How it works: Students prompt AI to generate questions about material they've studied, then close their devices completely before attempting to answer. Only after they've written or spoken their answers do they return to check accuracy—possibly by typing their answers in, recording a voice note, or taking a picture of what they've jotted down. They could even ask the AI to generate the ideal response, and check it manually against what they came up with.

Example prompt: *Generate 5 challenging questions about photosynthesis that require me to explain processes, not just recall facts. Focus on the light-dependent and light-independent reactions.*

Why it works: Students still do the effortful retrieval, but AI helps create better, more varied questions than they might generate themselves. The physical separation between question generation and answering prevents the temptation to peek.

Retrieval Strategy #2

The Confidence Calibration System

Metacognition and retrieval work hand-in-hand. This strategy makes that connection explicit.

How it works: After each retrieval attempt, students rate their confidence (1-5 scale) before checking their answer. They track patterns over time: When are they overconfident? Underconfident? Accurately calibrated? they can then share these patterns with the AI tool when it comes to reviewing a full topic or understanding what their overall understanding is.

Example process:

1. Student retrieves answer to question
2. Rates confidence: 'How sure am I this is correct?' (1-5)
3. Checks answer using AI or notes
4. Records: Was I right? Did my confidence match my accuracy?
5. AI helps identify patterns: e.g. *You're consistently overconfident about dates but underconfident about processes*

Why it works: This builds metacognitive awareness alongside content knowledge. Students learn to distinguish between genuine knowledge and the feeling of familiarity.

Retrieval Strategy #3

The Explanation Protocol

Move beyond factual retrieval into deeper understanding by having students explain concepts to AI that's programmed to be constructively confused.

How it works: Students explain a concept to AI that's been prompted to act like a curious but confused peer, asking clarifying questions when explanations are vague or incomplete.

Example prompt: *I'm going to explain how natural selection works. Act like a curious student who doesn't quite understand. Ask me specific questions if I'm vague, skip steps, or use terms without defining them. Don't correct me directly, just ask questions that make me think deeper.*

Why it works: This forces elaborative retrieval—students must not only remember but also organise and articulate their knowledge. The AI's questions reveal gaps they might not notice otherwise.

Retrieval Strategy #4

The Spaced Retrieval Calendar

Use AI to create a (hopefully!) optimised retrieval calendar that supports students to understand how and when to practice retrieving certain information.

How it works: Students input topics they need to learn, and AI creates a personalised retrieval schedule based on spacing research. Crucially, AI provides the schedule and questions, but students must do the actual retrieval without AI assistance.

Example prompt: *I need to memorise 20 key physics equations over the next 4 weeks. Create a spaced retrieval schedule that reviews each equation multiple times with increasing intervals. For each review session, just give me the prompt (like 'Write the equation for kinetic energy') not the answer.*

Why it works: This implements optimal spacing without requiring teachers (or students!) to manually track the schedules. It also allows for more time to be spent on the actual retrieval rather than on trying to craft the ideal schedule.

Retrieval Strategy #5

The Collaborative Retrieval Challenge

Use AI to facilitate peer retrieval practice without the social anxiety of public failure. Students can learn from one another and you don't risk the potential anti-social one-to-one AI conversations that might otherwise take over the classroom.

How it works: AI generates the same questions for pairs or small groups. Students first retrieve individually (in writing), then compare answers, then check against AI's feedback.

Example process:

1. AI generates question for all group members
2. Silent individual retrieval (2 minutes)
3. Compare answers in pairs (2 minutes)
4. Collaborative final answer (1 minute)
5. Check with AI for accuracy and completeness

Why it works: This combines the benefits of retrieval with elaborative discussion. Students see alternative ways of expressing knowledge and catch each other's mistakes before checking answers.

Retrieval Strategy #6

The Pre-emptive Retrieval Strike

Before students use AI for help with new work, require retrieval of relevant prior knowledge.

How it works: Build retrieval into the workflow whenever students need AI assistance. They must first attempt to recall related information before AI provides support.

Example process:

A student wants to ask AI for help with an essay on climate change:

1. They first write down everything they remember about greenhouse gases
2. They prompt AI: *I've recalled [lists what they remembered]. Now help me structure an essay on climate change impacts*
3. AI can build on what they retrieved, not replace it

Why it works: This prevents the blank-slate-to-AI pipeline that bypasses retrieval entirely. It also helps students see connections between prior knowledge and new tasks.

10

Spaced [ ] Repetition

If retrieval practice is about the *how* of remembering, spaced repetition is about the *when*. And it turns out that said 'when' matters enormously.

Here's a truth that might feel uncomfortable, particularly if you've got a sieve-like memory like me.

Forgetting is not a bug in the brain's system. It's a feature.

Our brains are designed to forget most of what we encounter, and that's actually brilliant—imagine if you remembered every car number plate you'd ever seen, every conversation you'd overheard on the bus, every random fact from every lesson you'd ever sat through. You'd be paralysed by irrelevance.

But this means that if we want students to remember something, we have to convince their brains it's worth keeping. And the way we do that isn't by hammering it home in one marathon session. It's by coming back to it, again and again, at increasingly spaced intervals. Each time we retrieve information after beginning to forget it, we send a signal: this matters, keep it accessible. And luckily for us, spaced repetition works perfectly with retrieval practice. Or, in other words, if we space out our retrieval just right, we might just hit the jackpot.

Again, the research is unequivocal: spreading practice over time leads to better long-term retention than massing it together, even when the total time spent is identical.

Let me put that more concretely. Take two students learning Spanish vocabulary. Student A studies for three hours on Sunday night. Student B studies for one hour on Monday, one on Wednesday, and one on Friday. Same three hours, radically different outcomes. Student B will remember significantly more a month later. Not slightly more—*significantly* more. Effect sizes in spacing research are consistently large enough to make educational researchers weep with joy.

When we space our practice, we allow some forgetting to occur between sessions. This makes the next retrieval more effortful—remember from the last chapter how effort strengthens memory? But there's more to it. Each time we successfully retrieve something after a delay, we're essentially telling our brain 'I needed this information again in a different context, at a different time, so you'd better keep it handy.' The memory trace doesn't just get stronger, it becomes more flexible and more accessible across different contexts. Recent research has added nuance to our understanding. The optimal spacing interval depends on how long you need to remember something for. If the test is in a week, review after a day or two. If it's in a month, space reviews across weeks. There's even a formula for it (though like all formulas in education, it's more guideline than gospel): the optimal gap between study sessions is about 10-20% of the retention interval you're aiming for.

Okay, now it's time to get on my preaching platform for just a moment... because here's the annoying thing: despite decades of evidence, spacing is rarely implemented well in schools. But it's not your fault!

Everything about how we structure education fights against spacing. Our classic Victorian-style curricula are designed like a conveyor belt—cover topic A, test it, move to topic B, never look back. Schemes of work march relentlessly forward. There's barely time to cover content once, let alone return to it systematically. When students do review, it's usually in frantic pre-exam cramming sessions, which we know feel productive but violates everything we know about how memory works.

Students actively resist spacing too, even when they know about it. A study from 2021 tracked 185 undergraduates using digital learning platforms. Despite having tools that encouraged spacing, most students massed their practice near deadlines. Only those who spaced their practice (and, handily enough for me trying to prove a point here, used retrieval practice as their main method) showed superior learning outcomes, despite investing the same total time as other students.

Why this resistance? Because spacing feels terrible whilst you're doing it. When you return to material after a gap, it feels harder than it did initially. That feeling of difficulty seems like failure—*I knew this last week, why can't I remember it now?* But that difficulty is precisely what makes spacing work. It's like the muscle soreness after exercise; it doesn't feel good, but it signals growth.

This connects directly back to our earlier discussions about metacognition. A strong metacognitive learner doesn't just monitor whether they know something; they understand the conditions under which that knowledge will remain accessible. They can resist the siren call of cramming because they understand it's a short-term fix with long-term costs.

But knowledge alone isn't enough. We need systems and structures that make spacing easier to implement than cramming. Which brings us to AI.

AI seems perfectly designed to solve the spacing problem. It can help students and teachers track learning, calculate optimal review intervals, generate practice questions at just the right moment, and adapt to individual forgetting curves. Platforms like Anki have been doing this using manual formulae for years with flashcards, but newer AI tools can help us do it with any content, in any format.

The promise is compelling: imagine every student having a personal AI tutor that knows exactly when they need to review each concept, that sends perfectly timed reminders, that makes spacing feel less like swimming upstream and more like following a gentle current.

But—and you *knew* there was a 'but' coming—the implementation matters enormously. Spacing only works if students are actually retrieving during those spaced intervals, not just re-exposing themselves to content. And this is where AI can accidentally sabotage the very thing it's trying to support.

Consider this scenario: An AI system reminds a student to review photosynthesis, which they studied two weeks ago. The student asks the AI to remind them about the structure of a plant cell versus an animal cell. The AI generates a beautiful summary. The student reads it, thinks *oh yes, I remember this,* and moves on. Has spacing occurred? Technically yes. Has learning been strengthened? Barely at all.

The problem is that AI makes it too easy to shift from retrieval to recognition, from active recall to passive review. The spacing might be perfect, but if the cognitive work has been outsourced to the AI, the benefit evaporates. Perhaps even more problematic is that many AI tools that purport to help with things like spaced repetition are paid or agentic, both of which are more difficult to access for students who may be under the recommended age of use, or not have the financial means to pay for a tool like that

So how *do* we harness AI's scheduling power whilst maintaining the cognitive effort that makes spacing effective, all in a way that is accessible to all students? The key is using AI to structure spacing whilst keeping the retrieval work firmly with the student.

So once again, let's jump into a few strategies that might help this work in the classroom. Use them in collaboration with the retrieval ones we looked at in the previous chapter, and you'll be well on your way!

* * *

Spaced Repetition Strategy #1

The Three-Touch Rule

Every key concept gets touched three times minimum: initial learning, review after 2-3 days, and review after 1-2 weeks. AI tracks what needs reviewing when, but students retrieve without assistance.

Implementation: Create a simple spreadsheet or use an existing tool to track:

- Topic introduced (date)
- First review due (date + 3 days)
- Second review due (date + 2 weeks)
- Third review due (date + 1 month)

Example prompt: *I taught [topic] on [date]. Generate three retrieval questions of increasing difficulty for reviews at 3 days, 2 weeks, and 1 month intervals.*

Why it works: This strategy exploits the forgetting curve at optimal intervals. After 2-3 days, students have begun to forget but haven't lost the material entirely—retrieval is effortful but achievable. After 2 weeks, more forgetting has occurred, making retrieval harder and therefore more beneficial. The month-long gap pushes the memory toward long-term storage.

Spaced Repetition Strategy #2

The Interleaved Review Session

Instead of reviewing one topic at a time, mix them up. This prevents students from using context as a crutch and strengthens discrimination between concepts.

Example process for a 10-minute review:

- Question from last lesson (2 mins)
- Question from last week (3 mins)
- Question from last month (3 mins)
- Connection question linking all three (2 mins)

Example prompt: *Generate a 10-minute review mixing questions from [Topic A - studied Monday], [Topic B - studied last week], and [Topic C - studied last month]. Include one question that connects all three.*

Why it works: When students study topics in blocks, they don't have to decide which strategy or concept applies—context does that for them. But interleaving removes those contextual scaffolds. This switching cost is a desirable difficulty that strengthens memory traces and improves transfer. The connection question at the end pushes students to see patterns across domains, building the kind of flexible thinking that defines expertise.

Spaced Repetition Strategy #3

The Confidence Tracker

Before each spaced review, students rate their confidence. After attempting retrieval, they rate their actual performance. Over time, they see the pattern: spaced practice feels harder but produces better results.

Example process:

1. AI presents topic for review
2. Student rates confidence (1-5)
3. Student attempts retrieval (no AI)
4. Student checks answer
5. Student rates actual performance (1-5)
6. AI tracks calibration accuracy over time

Why it works: Students develop metacognitive awareness about the relationship between feeling and knowing.

Spaced Repetition Strategy #4
The Cumulative Review Homework

Each homework assignment includes 70% new practice and 30% spaced review of previous topics.

Example process:

- Questions 1-7: Current topic practice
- Question 8: From last week's topic
- Question 9: From two weeks ago
- Question 10: From last month

Example Prompt: *Generate a homework assignment on [current topic] that includes 7 questions on new material and 3 spaced review questions from [previous topics and dates].*

Why it works: This strategy builds spacing into existing structures rather than adding extra work, making it sustainable for both teachers and students. The 70/30 split maintains focus on current learning whilst ensuring previous knowledge doesn't atro-

> phy. Students can't compartmentalise topics into 'done' and 'current'; everything remains active.

11

Weave in, Weave out: Interleaving

We've talked about retrieval (pulling things from memory) and spacing (when to do the pulling). Now it's time to look at how to organise that practice for maximum impact. Because it turns out that the comfortable, logical way we typically structure learning—finishing one topic completely before moving to the next—might *not* be the best way after all.

Here's a scenario every maths teacher will recognise: You're teaching quadratic equations. Students complete a worksheet with twenty quadratic problems. By problem fifteen, they're flying. By problem twenty, they've got it. You're satisfied. They're satisfied. Everyone feels that warm glow of mastery, and you all move on.

Fast forward two weeks. You slip a quadratic equation into a mixed review. The same students who were flying through problem twenty now stare blankly. "Miss, we haven't done these for ages!"

But you *have* done them. Twenty times in a row!

So what happened?

What happened is that blocked practice—doing the same type of problem repeatedly—created an illusion of learning. When students know the next problem will be quadratic, half the cognitive work is already done. They don't have to identify the problem type, select the appropriate strategy, or discriminate between approaches. They just apply the same procedure on autopilot. It feels like learning, but it's actually just repetition with training wheels.

On the other hand, interleaving is the practice of mixing different topics, problem types, or skills within a single study session rather than blocking them separately. Instead of all quadratics, then all linear equations, then all graphs, you'd mix them from the start. And the research on this is consistent: interleaving leads to better long-term retention and transfer, even though it feels harder and produces worse performance during practice. (And yes, I'm also noticing the trend here: learning is hard!)

The leading explanation for interleaving's effectiveness is the discrimination hypothesis. When topics are blocked, students don't need to figure out what kind of problem they're facing. Or in other words, if you give them a stack of quadratic-related questions, then they don't need to guess if they need the quadratic formula to answer them. But when topics are mixed, every problem becomes a two-part challenge: first identify what this is, then solve it.

This discrimination practice is crucial. In real life—and, let's be honest, in exam life too—problems don't usually come labelled. A student needs to recognise that this word problem requires algebra, not geometry. Or that this historical source needs contextualising within the Cold War, not World War II. This chemical reaction involves oxidation, not acid-base neutralisation. And so on, and so on.

Recent research adds further nuance to this by telling us that interleaving works best when the mixed topics are superficially similar but require different underlying strategies. Mixing quadratics with linear equations (both look like maths problems but need different approaches) is more beneficial than mixing quadratics with French vocabulary (obviously different categories).

The brain needs to work to discriminate, but the discrimination needs to be meaningful. Which means of course we have yet another connection back to metacognition! Every time students encounter a new problem in an interleaved sequence, they must:

- Pause and assess what type of problem this is
- Search their memory for the appropriate strategy
- Apply that strategy
- Evaluate whether it worked

This is exactly what we looked at when we defined metacognition through the lens of the EEF: planning, monitoring, evaluating. Interleaving therefore builds the executive function skills that separate surface learning from deep understanding.

Students who regularly experience interleaved practice become better at recognising patterns, selecting strategies, and monitoring their own understanding. They develop 'adaptive expertise,' or the ability to flexibly apply knowledge in novel situations. In our AI age, where information is always available but knowing what to do with it isn't, this kind of flexible thinking becomes even more crucial.

If I'm being honest, though, interleaving can be annoying. It's a lot easier for students just to block focus on one topic at a time. It's a lot easier for teachers to give topic-specific revision sessions or resources. It takes time to work out how to do it, more time to work out how to do it well, and more time to prove that, yes, it actually *is* working, even though it feels like it isn't!

This is where AI enters the picture. AI could be the tool that finally makes interleaving practical at scale. After all, consider the possibilities. AI could:

- Generate endless interleaved practice sets tailored to individual students, ages, or classes
- Adjust the mixture based on uploaded (and, of course, anonymised!) performance data
- Create connections between seemingly disparate topics

But here's the catch: AI's default mode is often to organise, categorise, and simplify. Ask an AI tool for for practice problems, and it will likely give you neat categories. Request a study guide, and it will probably block topics logically. The efficiency we love in AI can work against the productive messiness of interleaving.

So how do we get it to work properly?

Good prompting is key if we want good interleaving. Again I've opted to be subject-specific in the examples you're about to see, so that you can get an idea of what a good prompt might look like. Simply change the existing key words, age groups, and topics to best fit your context!

* * *

Interleaving Strategy #1

The Daily Mixed Starter

Begin each lesson with 3-5 questions mixing current and previous topics. No labels, no hints about problem type.

How to do it: Use AI to generate a brief starter activity that forces students to identify what type of problem they're facing before solving it. Display questions one at a time to prevent scanning ahead for context clues.

Example prompts:

- *Create 5 quick questions mixing topics from the last two weeks of [Year 9 science]: [cells], [energy transfers], and [chemical reactions]. Don't label which is which.*
- *Generate a 5-minute starter with problems from [fractions], [algebra], and [percentages]. Include one trick question where the obvious method isn't the correct one.*
- *Give me 4 mixed questions from our [Tudor history] unit covering [political changes], [religious reforms], and [social structure]. Students should need different types of historical thinking for each.*

Why it works: Students start each lesson practising discrimination, the core cognitive skill that makes interleaving effective.

Interleaving Strategy #2

The Homework Scrambler

Transform traditional blocked homework into interleaved practice without creating new resources.

How to do it: Take your existing homework problems and use AI to strategically reorder them. Ensure no two consecutive problems use the same method or concept. Add a requirement for students to identify the problem type before solving.

Example prompts:

- *Here are 15 [maths] problems grouped by type: [list them]. Reorganise so no two consecutive problems use the same method. Add a 'problem type' box before each question.*
- *Take these [10 chemistry questions] about [acids, bases, and salts]. Mix them up and add distractor questions that look similar but require different approaches.*
- *Scramble these [French grammar exercises] covering [passé composé], [futur proche], and [subjonctif]. Ensure each tense appears at least twice but never consecutively.*

Why it works: This maintains the same content coverage whilst adding discrimination practice. The cognitive effort shifts from repetitive application to active decision-making about which strategy to use. Students can't rely on mental momentum from the previous problem.

Interleaving Strategy #3

The Comparison Generator

Use AI to create problems that look similar but require different approaches.

How to do it: Have AI generate pairs or triplets of problems with similar surface features but different underlying structures. Students must first identify which approach each problem needs, then solve them.

Example prompts:

- *Generate 3 pairs of [physics] problems that look similar but require different approaches: one using [conservation of energy], one using [force equations]. Make the differences subtle.*
- *Create 5 [history] source analysis questions where sources look similar but require different analytical frameworks: [bias analysis], [contextualisation], or [corroboration].*
- *Write pairs of [word problems] where one requires [multiplication] and one requires [division], but both use similar language and numbers.*

Why it works: This directly trains the discrimination skills that separate novices from experts. Students learn to look beyond surface features to underlying structure. The comparison forces explicit attention to what makes problems different despite appearances.

Interleaving Strategy #4

The Topic Fade Method

Instead of abruptly ending topics, fade them into ongoing practice over weeks.

How to do it: When finishing a topic, systematically include questions from it in subsequent homework and classwork. Start with 30% old topic, 70% new, then gradually decrease the percentage (but never to zero—remember Ebbinghaus' curve of forgetting!).

Example prompts:

- *Create a homework set with [70% questions on current topic - photosynthesis] and [30% on last week's topic - respiration]. Mix them throughout.*
- *Generate 10 practice problems: [5 on this week's topic - quadratics], [3 on last week's - linear equations], [2 on topic from three weeks ago - inequalities].*
- *Design a worksheet that includes [current topic - WW2] as the main focus but weaves in questions from [previous topic - WW1] and [earlier topic - interwar period] for comparison.*

Why it works: This combines interleaving with spacing, preventing knowledge from becoming inert. Students maintain retrieval practice across topics whilst building discrimination skills.

The gradual fade mimics how knowledge needs to remain accessible over time, not just immediately after learning.

Interleaving Strategy #5

The Progressive Difficulty Scramble

Mix topics whilst gradually increasing complexity across the practice session.

How to do it: Have AI create mixed problem sets where difficulty increases but topics remain varied. Each "level" contains different topics, preventing students from using difficulty as a cue for problem type.

Example prompts:

- *Create 12 questions mixing [algebra], [geometry], and [statistics]. Group into 4 difficulty levels with 3 questions each (one per topic). Mix topics within each level.*
- *Generate a progressive practice set for [Spanish]: Level 1 mixes [basic vocabulary] from [family], [school], and [food] topics. Level 2 mixes [sentence construction] from the same topics. Level 3 requires [paragraph writing].*

- *Build a stepped challenge mixing [Biology topics]: [cells], [genetics], and [ecology]. Start with recall questions, move to application, end with analysis. Keep topics mixed throughout.*

Why it works: This maintains appropriate challenge whilst preventing students from using difficulty as a shortcut to identify problem types. The progression builds confidence whilst maintaining discrimination practice

12

I challenge you to a Dual... Coding

Years ago, when I was still teaching history, I fell in love with timelines. Not the clean, professionally printed ones—I mean the scrappy, hand-drawn ones on the board. I'd use whatever colour markers I could find and sketch out a wobbly line across the whiteboard, placing key events along it with stick figures, squiggly arrows, and dodgy attempts at battle scenes. I'm not great at drawing. In fact, I'd often joke with students that my version of a horse looked more like a melting dog. But that didn't matter. If anything, the worse the drawings were, the more students remembered them. "That was the lesson where Bismarck looked like a potato," one student once said to me—and weirdly, she also remembered the political alliances we covered in the lesson.

Now, this wasn't a Bob Ross-style 'happy little accident.' I was using what I'd learned from practitioners such as Oliver Caviglioli to combine verbal explanation with visual representation for better cognition. Or, in other words, I was dual coding my timelines.

Let's clear something up straight away: dual coding has nothing to do with learning styles. I know, I know, you've probably sat through a million CPD sessions about visual learners and auditory learners and kinaesthetic learners. It's intuitive, it's popular, and it's comprehensively debunked. Matching instruction to supposed learning styles doesn't improve outcomes. What *does* improve outcomes is giving all students multiple representations of information.

Dual coding theory, developed by Allan Paivio in the 1970s and refined ever since, suggests we process verbal and visual information through separate but interconnected channels. Words (spoken or written) go through one system, images through another. When information comes through both channels and those channels reference each other, we create multiple retrieval routes to the same knowledge.

Think of it like this: if memory is a library, dual coding means filing the same book in two different sections with cross-references between them. You can find it by looking up words or by browsing images. Double the access points, and you make the memory stronger.

The research support is overwhelming. In 1992, Mayer and Anderson found students who received animation alongside narration learned problem-solving procedures better than those with animation or narration alone. More recently, studies show dual coding improves learning across subjects, ages, and abilities—from primary school to higher education.

But why does it work?

Go back to what you know about working memory. We learned, in the story of SLOB, that working memory has a limited capacity. Here's the fun bit that we didn't cover, though: that limit applies separately to verbal and visual channels. By using both at the same time, we're essentially doubling our processing capacity without overload.

But it's not just about capacity. When verbal and visual information complement each other, they create 'referential connections'.

The term 'absolute monarchy' connects to a diagram of England in the 1600s. The diagram triggers recall of the word. Each strengthens the other. It's the cognitive equivalent of ice dancers picking up ballroom—different exercises strengthening the same underlying fitness.

Now connect that to what we've discussed about retrieval practice. When students draw a concept from memory, they're retrieving twice—once to recall the information, once to translate it visually. When they explain a diagram verbally, same thing in reverse. The act of translation between modes is itself a form of elaborative retrieval.

The most powerful dual coding happens when students generate their own visuals, not just consume pre-made ones. This taps into the generation effect; we remember better what we create ourselves.

Here's an example: when students draw their own diagram of the water cycle, they're doing several things simultaneously:

1. Retrieving information about the water cycle
2. Deciding what's important enough to include
3. Figuring out spatial relationships between elements
4. Creating visual metaphors for abstract processes
5. Connecting verbal labels to visual elements

That's five different types of cognitive work from one drawing task! Compare that to looking at a textbook diagram, where the cognitive work is... recognising that rain falls downward.

There's one more thing to consider: bad drawing leads to good learning. In fact, there's evidence that overly polished visuals can actually hinder learning through because students get distracted by aesthetics rather than focusing on meaning.

My terrible timeline drawings worked because:

- Students had to actively interpret them (more cognitive work)
- The imperfection made them less intimidating to recreate
- The humour created an emotional hook for memory
- Students felt permission to create their own bad drawings

That last point matters enormously. When students see perfect textbook diagrams, they often think 'I could never create that.' When they see their teacher's wonky stick figures explaining the feudal system, they think 'I could do better than that.' And then they do. And in doing so, they learn.

Enter AI, which can generate stunning visuals from simple text prompts. A student types *diagram of the heart* and gets a medical-quality illustration in seconds (although how accurate it is might be up for question!). A teacher requests 'timeline of the Cold War' and receives something that would've taken hours to create manually.This is simultaneously wonderful and dangerous.

It's wonderful because:

- Teac hers with limited artistic skills can provide visual representations
- Students can quickly visualise complex ideas
- Multiple representations can be generated and compared
- Accessibility improves for students who struggle with drawing

But then it becomes dangerous because:

- The cognitive work of translation vanishes
- Students consume rather than create

- The generation effect disappears
- Pretty pictures replace effortful processing

So as always, the key question isn't 'Should we use AI for visuals?' but 'How do we use AI to enhance rather than replace the cognitive work of dual coding?'

Strategies abound!

* * *

Dual Coding Strategy #1

The One-Minute Sketch

Students have 60 seconds to sketch a concept from memory. No notes, no AI, just brain to paper.

How to do it: At the end of a lesson segment, give students 'sketch time'. Limit the timing here! Students draw the key concept just covered. Share sketches in pairs, explaining what each element represents. Then use AI to generate a 'professional' version and compare. More advanced classes or concepts might benefit from analysis and pulling the AI up on its mistakes or omissions.

Why it works: The time pressure prevents perfectionism, forcing students to identify essential elements. The retrieval from memory strengthens encoding. Comparing with AI output afterwards highlights gaps and misconceptions whilst validating student understanding, and also gets them used to questioning the reliability of AI image outputs, something that we don't always do.

Dual Coding Strategy #2

The Visual Summary Challenge

Transform verbal notes into visual summaries, using a combination of student drawing and AI support.

How to do it: Students review their written notes and create a one-page visual summary using drawings, diagrams, and minimal text. They can use AI to generate specific elements they can't draw, but must arrange and connect them manually.

Why it works: Students must identify key information, determine relationships, and create visual metaphors. The combination of hand-drawing and AI generation maintains cognitive effort whilst removing artistic barriers.

Dual Coding Strategy #3

The Diagram Annotation Workout

Start with AI-generated diagrams and transform them through annotation and modification.

How to do it: Generate a basic diagram using AI, then have students correct mistakes and add layers of information through annotation. Each addition requires retrieval and connection-making.

Why it works: Students engage with pre-made visuals actively rather than passively. The annotation requires retrieval and integration of verbal knowledge with visual representation. Multiple passes deepen processing and again ensure they don't take AI at face value.

Dual Coding Strategy #4

The Visual Vocabulary Builder

Create visual dictionaries where each term has both verbal and visual definitions.

How to do it: For new vocabulary, students create three elements: written definition, hand-drawn symbol, and AI-generated image. They then explain connections between all three.

Why it works: Multiple representations create multiple retrieval routes. The act of creating connections between representations deepens understanding. The mix of hand-drawing and AI maintains effort whilst ensuring clarity.

Dual Coding Strategy #5
The Explanation Flip

Students alternate between explaining visuals verbally and creating visuals from verbal descriptions.

How to do it: Partner work where Student A explains an AI-generated diagram without showing it, Student B draws based on description, then compare and discuss differences.

Why it works: Forces precise verbal description and careful visual interpretation. Mismatches reveal misconceptions and/or AI inaccuracies. The translation between modes strengthens both channels.

13

Well Whaddya Know? Prior Knowledge Activation

Here's a conversation I once overheard between two Year 7 students using an AI tool to work on their history homework:

"Ask it about the causes of World War One."

"I did. It's just listing loads of countries and dates."

"What about the assassination?"

"What's an assassination?"

"When the guy killed the Archduke. You know, with the sandwich?"

"How do I ask about something when I don't know what it's called?"

And there it is. The fundamental problem with expecting AI to solve our learning challenges: you can't look up what you don't know exists. Or, in the words of an amazing leader I once worked under, "You don't know what you don't know." You can't ask questions about concepts you've never encountered. You can't make connections to knowledge you don't have.

This isn't a limitation of AI. It's once again a feature of how our brains work. And understanding it might be the difference between AI enhancing education and AI creating an even wider achievement gap.

You see, every piece of new learning needs somewhere to land. When I tell you that 'the mitochondria is the powerhouse of the cell,' that information only sticks if you already know what a cell is, what 'powerhouse' means metaphorically, and why cells might need energy. Without that foundation, it's just noise.

These are forms of schemas, which I've already mentioned a few times in this book. Schemas are a bit like mental filing systems. When new information arrives, we file it into existing folders, creating connections and cross-references. But if there's no relevant folder? The information has nowhere to go. It floats briefly in working memory, then disappears.

This is what E.D. Hirsch means when he says "it takes knowledge to gain knowledge." The more you know, the easier it becomes to learn more. The less you know, the harder everything becomes. Studies show that when experts and novices look up the same information, experts learn more from it. Not because they're smarter, but because they have frameworks to slot new information into. An expert physicist reading about a new particle can immediately connect it to existing knowledge about forces, energy, and quantum mechanics. Meanwhile, a novice is trying to understand what a particle even *is.*

Putting this into a school context, it won't be news to you to find that students with strong prior knowledge acquire new information easily, while those with gaps struggle increasingly over time.

Consider vocabulary. Research shows that by age three, children from professional families have heard 30 million more words than children from disadvantaged backgrounds. By secondary school, an advantaged 17-year-old knows approximately 80,000 words. That's roughly 13 new words learned every day since age one. A disadvantaged student might know 40,000.

Now imagine both students ask ChatGPT to explain climate change. The AI responds with a perfectly pitched explanation involving greenhouse gases, atmospheric pressure, thermal radiation, and feedback loops. The student with 80,000 words understands most of this, maybe needing to clarify one or two terms. The student with 40,000 words is lost by the second sentence.

The AI can't fix this.

In fact, it might make it worse.

Let me give you another example. When my colleague's Year 3 class used a chatbot to 'interview' an ancient Roman, the successful interactions came from students who already knew enough to ask interesting questions. They knew Romans had different technology, so they asked about engineering. They knew about social hierarchy, so they asked about slaves and citizens. One great exchange started with 'Where did you poo?'—a brilliant (and amusing) question that led that student to learning about aqueducts and public health, but only because the student already understood that Romans wouldn't have had modern plumbing.

The students who struggled? They didn't know what they didn't know. They asked "What's your name?" and "What's your favourite colour?" They got answers, but learned nothing meaningful because they lacked the framework to make those answers significant.

If we go back again to retrieval practice, we find that prior knowledge is apparent even there. You can't retrieve what was never properly encoded. And proper encoding requires connecting to existing knowledge. AI can provide information, but it can't create the initial connections that make that information meaningful.

Vocabulary deserves special attention because it's the gateway to all other learning. Research suggests you need to understand about 95% of the words in a text to learn from it effectively. Below that threshold, comprehension collapses.

Think about what this means for AI-augmented learning. Every AI explanation, no matter how well-crafted, is made of words. If students don't know those words, the explanation is useless. Worse, AI tends to use precise, academic vocabulary—exactly the language that disadvantaged students are less likely to know.

There's one more thing for us to think about when it comes to prior knowledge: *activation.* Prior knowledge isn't just about having information; it's about activating it at the right moment. Knowledge can be present but dormant. Students might know relevant information but not realise it's relevant.

This is where skillful teaching becomes crucial. Before students engage with new content—whether from AI or traditional sources—they need their relevant prior knowledge activated. They need to be reminded of what they already know that connects to what they're about to learn.

It turns out, maybe AI can help with prior knowledge, after all. When used right, AI can become your prior knowledge activation engine. And, best of all, it puts all the thinking right in the hands of the students, not the machine.

* * *

Prior Knowledge Activation Strategy #1

The Knowledge Audit

Before introducing new topics, systematically assess and activate what students already know.

How to do it: Use AI to generate a quick diagnostic that reveals existing knowledge and gaps. Students complete it individually, then discuss in pairs what they knew, what surprised them, and what they want to learn.

Example prompts:

- *Create a 10 question diagnostic quiz about [the water cycle] that checks if students understand [states of matter], [temperature], and [the sun's role].*
- *Generate 'agree or disagree' statements about [World War 2] that will reveal whether students understand [the interwar period], [European geography], and [20th century technology].*
- *Design a concept mapping starter where students connect terms related to [cells] to show their existing understanding of [living things], [microscopes], and [organisation levels].*

Why it works: Makes existing knowledge visible to both teacher and students. Reveals gaps that need filling before new learning can succeed. Activates dormant knowledge that might otherwise remain unconnected.

Prior Knowledge Activation Strategy #2

The Vocabulary Front-Load

Pre-teach essential vocabulary before content delivery, using AI to identify and explain key terms.

How to do it: Have AI analyse your lesson content and identify vocabulary that students must understand. Teach these words explicitly before the main lesson, using AI to generate examples and non-examples and building this into a visual diagram such as a Frayer model.

Example prompts:

- *Analyse this text about [photosynthesis]. List the 10 most important vocabulary words students need to know. For each, provide a student-friendly definition, an example, and a non-example.*
- *Generate a vocabulary pre-teaching activity for [Shakespeare's Macbeth Act 1]. Include [modern translations], [visual representations], and [contemporary analogies].*
- *Create a graduated vocabulary ladder for [quadratic equations], starting with terms Year 7s would know and building to Year 10 level. Use the attached unit plan as a guide.*

Why it works: Removes vocabulary as a barrier to learning. Ensures all students have linguistic access to content. Creates shared classroom language that enables discussion.

Prior Knowledge Activation Strategy #3

The Bridge Builder

Explicitly connect new learning to familiar experiences and knowledge.

How to do it: Before teaching new content, use AI to generate analogies and connections to students' likely prior experiences. Have students evaluate which connections work best for them.

Example prompts:

- *Generate 5 different analogies for [electrical circuits] using everyday experiences like [water pipes], [traffic], [postal systems]. Show how each analogy helps and where it breaks down.*
- *Create connections between [the feudal system] and modern experiences students would understand like [school hierarchies], [social media influencers], [esports].*
- *Link [protein synthesis] to familiar processes like [following a recipe], [building with Lego], [copying a playlist]. Explain what aspects each analogy captures.*

Why it works: Makes abstract concepts concrete by connecting to existing schemas. Provides multiple access points for different students. Shows that new learning builds on what they already know. Models ways students could use AI to support their own understanding!

Prior Knowledge Activation Strategy #4

The Misconception Hunt

Surface and address incorrect prior knowledge before it interferes with new learning.

How to do it: Use AI to generate common misconceptions about your topic. Have students identify which they believe, discuss why these seem logical, then provide evidence for correct understanding.

Example prompts:

- *List 5 common misconceptions students have about [evolution]. For each, explain [why it seems logical], [what's actually wrong], and [the correct understanding].*
- *Generate believable but incorrect statements about [gravity] that reveal typical student misunderstandings. Include explanations of why these misconceptions persist.*
- *Create a 'myth busters' activity about [medieval life] addressing misconceptions from popular media. Show what students likely believe versus historical reality.*

Why it works: Incorrect prior knowledge actively interferes with new learning. Addressing misconceptions explicitly prevents them from distorting new information. This one also shows students that revising understanding is part of learning.

Prior Knowledge Activation Strategy #5

The Progressive Disclosure

Build complex understanding by gradually layering new information onto solid foundations.

How to do it: Use AI to break complex topics into prerequisite knowledge chunks. Teach and verify understanding of each layer before adding the next.

Example prompts:

- *Break down [photosynthesis] into 5 levels of understanding, from Year 7 to 11. Show what prior knowledge each level requires.*
- *Create a learning progression for [World War 1 causes] that builds from [understanding what countries are] to [analysing complex alliance systems].*
- *Design a stepped approach to teaching [algebra] to [Year 9] that identifies and builds on required prior knowledge at each stage.*

Why it works: Ensures foundational knowledge is solid before building complexity. Prevents cognitive overload by managing the knowledge load. Makes learning feel achievable by showing clear progression.

From Anti-Cheating to Pro-Thinking

14

Why Detection is a Losing Game

Let me tell you about the most dispiriting conversation I had last year. A colleague had just spent days—*days*!—trying to determine whether a student had used AI for their coursework. They'd run it through four different detection tools (all gave different results), compared it to the student's previous work (inconclusive), and even tried reverse-engineering prompts that might have produced it (got close but not quite).

A huge amount of their teaching week had gone to playing detective instead of teaching. Meanwhile, that student had probably already submitted three more assignments, each one harder to detect than the last. And even if my colleague *was* right, what had we actually achieved? We'd caught one instance of misuse whilst teaching the student to be sneakier next time.

And here's the thing people don't seem to be understanding: we've already lost the detection war. AI detection tools are, at best, educated guesswork. At worst? They're actively harmful.

The technical reality is sobering. Current detection tools work by identifying patterns they associate with AI writing—certain phrase structures, vocabulary choices, syntactic patterns. But the problem is that these patterns often overlap with good student writing. I've seen detection tools flag:

- EAL students for 'unusual' phrasing that's just non-standard English
- Neurodiverse students for 'repetitive structures' that help them organise their thoughts
- High-achieving students for 'sophistication beyond expected level'
- and... the Bible. For some unknown reason.

Meanwhile, students who actually use AI are learning to evade detection with laughable ease. They're asking AI tools to:

- Write like a tired 16-year-old
- Include some grammatical mistakes
- Make it sound like someone who half-understood the topic
- Use simpler vocabulary throughout

So now we're not just failing to catch cheating, we're teaching students to deliberately worsen their work. If that's not educational malpractice, I don't know what is.

And the technical failure of detection tools isn't even the biggest problem! The real damage is what it's doing to the teacher-student relationship.

Every time we run work through a detector, we send a message: 'I don't trust you'. Every accusation based on algorithmic suspicion, every confrontation about how *this doesn't sound like you,* every request to *prove this is your work*—it all adds up to an adversarial dynamic that poisons learning.

I've watched this poison spread through departments and seen multiple stories online from students this has happened to. Teachers become suspicious of improvement ('too good to be true'). Students become paranoid about success ('what if they think I cheated?'). Parents get involved, demanding either stricter detection or protection from false accusations. Everyone's exhausted, everyone's angry, and nobody's actually learning anything.

We're still trying to chase students for cheating on their work, when 'cheating' just doesn't mean the same thing anymore—and without ever really thinking about why it's happening in the first place.

Oh look, it's the perfect time for a personal confession:

Let me take you back to Year 8 Social Studies, early 2000s, with little Amelia in a panic. Major homework due; multi-page report with maps and research. And I hadn't done it. Not started it, not thought about it, completely dropped the ball.

My friends handed theirs into the dropbox outside our classroom. I told them I'd handed mine in earlier. For a week, I pushed down the growing fear.

Now, a bit of context: I was *that* student. You know, the one who was always on time, loved school, good relationships with teachers. Not handing in an assignment and then lying about it wasn't me.

Except, apparently, it was.

A week later, assignments were returned. The teacher stopped at my desk: "Amelia, I seem to be missing yours?"

"Oh, that's weird. I definitely handed it in!"

The teacher paused. He was not the most organised—his desk was legendary for its chaos. So it was entirely plausible my work got lost in the archaeological layers of unmarked papers. More plausible than me, straight-A reliable Amelia, lying to his face.

Long story short: I got a profuse apology for his 'carelessness' and a grade based on 'what you would have received, based on previous work.' Near top of the class. My parents saw another glowing report. I never told anyone the truth.

Until now. Cue dramatic music.

I'm sharing this because it illuminates something crucial: cheating isn't really about character. I wasn't a 'bad' student. I wasn't lazy or dishonest by nature. I was a thirteen-year-old who'd made a mistake, then made a worse mistake trying to cover it up.

The system I was in—one built on compliance, grades, and reputation, and the same one that schools still largely operate in today—made lying feel safer than admitting failure.

When we build academic integrity around catching cheaters, we teach toxic lessons:

- Success = not getting caught
- Teachers = adversaries to outsmart
- Learning = performance for grades
- Mistakes = dangerous admissions

These lessons were problematic with paper assignments. With AI, they're catastrophic. Because now students have a perfect accomplice—one that never judges, never reports, and never refuses to help them avoid the shame of struggle.

* * *

Before we can address AI misuse, we need to understand why students turn to it. And please, let's move past 'because they can' or 'kids today are lazy.' That's not analysis; it's abdication.

The reality is far more complex and far more human. Take a model Year 12 student; conscientious, generally engaged. She used ChatGPT for a history essay last week, and when you talked about it, she nearly cried. Not from guilt, but from exhaustion. That particular week, she had three coursework deadlines colliding, two group projects where she was carrying teammates who'd bailed on her, a part-time job she couldn't afford to quit, and caring responsibilities for younger siblings whilst her mum worked nights. By the time she sat down to write about Mussolini's militaristic strengths at 11 PM on Tuesday, she wasn't thinking about academic integrity. She was thinking about survival.

Then there's the anxiety piece, which I think we massively underestimate. I've watched genuinely capable students spiral into panic over assignments that should be well within their abilities. Picture a Year 10 student—straight grade 9s, crushing pressure from home—who tells you that they've written and deleted the same introduction seventeen times. Each attempt felt worse than the last. His parents had hired a tutor after his last essay got a grade 7 instead of an 8. The message was clear: anything less than perfect meant failure. He admits to you that, at midnight, with the deadline looming, he turned to ChatGPT. Not because he couldn't do the work, but because he was terrified of doing it imperfectly. AI offered something his anxiety couldn't: guaranteed competence. His finished work might not be brilliant, but it wouldn't be embarrassing. The tragic irony is that his own attempts were probably better than what the AI produced, but perfectionism had made that impossible to see.

Or how about the relevance void, which is one I'm sure you've seen plenty of times regardless of what you teach. When students can't see why their work matters, outsourcing it to AI becomes entirely logical. Imagine the conversation with a student who has used AI for a persuasive essay about, let's say, school uniform policy. When asked if she cared about uniform rules, she looks at you like you're mad. "Nobody cares about uniform rules," she says. "We're just pretending to have opinions for marks." And she's right, of course. We're asking her to fake passion for fake purposes that would be read by one person and then forgotten. In her mind, using AI to generate empty arguments for an empty exercise was simply efficiency. Why waste genuine thought on something that doesn't warrant it?

And then there's the skills gap, which can link further to what we looked at in the last chapter about prior knowledge and not knowing what you don't know. Some students want to do the work but literally don't know how. They understand the content but not the process. A Year 11 student, for example, bright and engaged, who completely understood Macbeth's themes but had no idea how to structure that understanding into an essay. Nobody had ever explicitly taught him how to build an argument, how to integrate quotations, how to transition between ideas. The gap between the ideas in his head and the essay on the page felt insurmountable. AI bridges that gap instantly. He wasn't avoiding thinking; he was compensating for skills we'd assumed he had but never actually taught.

Let's zoom out further. Students see adults using AI for everything:

- Emails written by ChatGPT
- Presentations designed by Gamma
- Code generated by Claude
- Art created by Midjourney

The message? Efficiency trumps process. Results matter more than method. Time saved is value created.

Then we're shocked when students apply this same logic to their learning? We've spent decades teaching them that grades matter more than growth, that performance beats process, that the point is to get things done, not to think deeply. AI is just revealing contradictions that were always there. So, in my opinion at least, here's the mindset shift we need: instead of asking 'how do we stop students from cheating?' we should ask 'why would students want to think for themselves?'

You see, AI stops being a replacement and starts being a tool only when we create conditions where thinking is rewarding, where struggle is safe, and where learning connects to things that matter. This isn't me being naively optimistic. It's strategic realism. We can't win an arms race against AI. Detection will always lag behind generation. Students will always find workarounds—they always have done! And the technology (and the way they use it!) will always evolve faster than our policies.

But we can win by changing the game entirely.

A brief interlude

What changing the game actually looks like

From Surveillance to Relationship

Instead of: Running work through detectors
Try: Regular conversations about thinking processes

Instead of: "This doesn't sound like you"
Try: "Walk me through how you approached this"

Instead of: Gotcha moments
Try: Curious exploration of student reasoning

From Compliance to Engagement

Instead of: Generic assignments that anyone could complete
Try: Personal investigations that require individual perspective

Instead of: Single-attempt, high-stakes assessments
Try: Iterative work that builds over time

Instead of: Hidden rubrics and mysterious standards
Try: Co-created success criteria that students understand

From Fear to Growth
Instead of: Punishing mistakes
Try: Celebrating productive struggle

Instead of: Perfection as the standard
Try: Progress as the measure

Instead of: Answers as endpoints
Try: Questions as beginnings

My Year 8 homework lie wasn't really about homework. It was about a system that made admitting struggle feel more dangerous than living with deception. Twenty-odd years later, we're still operating that same system, just with better technology for both cheating and catching.

The solution isn't better detection. It's better education. It's creating classrooms where:

- Thinking is genuinely more interesting than copying
- Struggle is seen as strength, not weakness
- Work connects to things students actually care about
- The process genuinely matters more than the product
- Students have the skills to tackle challenges confidently

When we get this right, AI becomes what it should be: a thinking partner, not a thinking replacement. Students still use it, but they use it to enhance their ideas, not to avoid having them.

So, let's talk about cheese.

15

The Swiss Cheese Model

I'm about to steal something from the aviation safety department, and I promise it's relevant to your Year 9s who keep submitting ChatGPT's thoughts on Romeo and Juliet.

In 1990, James Reason gave us the Swiss Cheese Model of accident causation. The idea is beautifully simple: no single safety measure is perfect. Every defence has holes, like a slice of Swiss cheese. A pilot might miss a warning light. Air traffic control might misread altitude. Weather radar might glitch. Each slice has holes, but stack them together and the holes rarely align. When disaster strikes in aviation, it's usually because multiple failures lined up perfectly—all the holes aligned and danger slipped through.

Here's why this matters for us: we keep trying to find the one perfect solution to AI misuse. The unbeatable detector. The AI-proof assignment. The foolproof policy. But that's not how complex problems work. There is no single solution because there's no single problem.

Instead, we need layers. Multiple imperfect barriers that, together, create something robust. Not because any one layer is bulletproof, but because when a student slips through one, another catches them.

More importantly, when designed right, it's becomes less about catching cheaters and more about removing the desire to cheat in the first place.

* * *

Layer 1: Culture (Making Thinking Visible and Celebrated)

The first slice of cheese isn't a rule or a tool. It's a culture shift. We need classrooms where the thinking process is more valued than the final product.

This sounds lovely in theory, but what does it actually look like? Imagine starting class not with 'Who finished their essay?' but with 'Who got properly stuck yesterday and how did you get unstuck?' Culture shifts are all about finding the points when struggle becomes the interesting part, when false starts are worth sharing, when confusion is seen as the beginning of understanding rather than evidence of failure.

The key is genuinely getting interested in how students think, not just what they produce. When a student explains their reasoning—even if they reached the wrong conclusion—we learn more about their understanding than any final answer could tell us. It's the difference between asking "What's the answer?" and asking "Walk me through how you approached this."

Consider getting students to keep 'thinking logs' alongside traditional assignments. Not formal academic reflections, just quick notes: *Started by thinking X, but then realised Y. Got stuck on Z for ages until I remembered that thing about Q.* These process documents become as valuable as the work itself. The nice thing about it is that you can't fake authentic confusion. You can't outsource your own moments of clarity to AI.

Classroom Connections

1. The Thinking Timeline

Have students create a visual timeline of their thinking process for any assignment. Not a content timeline—a thinking timeline.

- When did they start?
- When did they get stuck?
- When did breakthrough moments happen?
- What triggered shifts in understanding?

Students present these alongside their work, and suddenly the journey becomes as interesting as the destination. You can't fake the authentic moments of 'spent 20 minutes convinced I was right, then realised I'd misread the question entirely... oops.'

2. Confusion of the Week

End each week by having students nominate their Best Confusion: the moment where they were most productively lost. Make it competitive:

- Who got confused in the most interesting way?

- Who's confusion led to the biggest breakthrough?
- Who had the most unique confusion, and what can we all learn from it?

Create a wall of fame for excellent confusions—digital, by post-it note, or any other method, as long as it's public. When confusion becomes a badge of honour rather than shame, students stop wanting to skip straight to answers.

3. Process Interviews

Pair students up and have them interview each other about their work using only "how" and "why" questions.

- How did you decide to start with that point?
- Why did you change your approach halfway through?
- How did you make the leap from this part to this part?

The interviewer takes notes and submits them alongside the work. These peer observations often reveal thinking that students themselves aren't even conscious of—and they're impossible to generate with AI.

Layer 2: Assessment Design (Making AI Use More Trouble Than It's Worth)

The second slice is about clever task design. Not 'AI-proof' tasks—that's impossible. Instead, it's about creating tasks where using AI thoughtlessly actually makes the work harder.

Think about assignments that require such specific, personal context that by the time you've explained everything to AI, you've essentially done the thinking yourself. How would a historical event have affected your specific street? What mathematical formula explains your particular morning routine? Which character in the novel most reminds you of someone in your family and why?

The magic here isn't that AI can't do these tasks. If you give it enough information, it probably could. The magic is that gathering and explaining that information requires the same cognitive work as doing the assignment yourself. You end up writing the essay in the prompt itself.

Or consider incremental work that builds over time. Initial position on Monday. Counter-argument that made you reconsider on Wednesday. Refined position on Friday. New complicating evidence next Monday. Each step builds on the last, requiring consistency and development. Sure, AI could handle each stage, but maintaining coherence across all of them? That's more work than just thinking it through yourself.

Another approach: assignments rooted in genuine annoyance or curiosity. Create a mathematical model for something that personally frustrates you. Write a persuasive piece about a hyper-local issue only you and your neighbours care about. Analyse a text through the lens of your own specific expertise or hobby. AI can generate generic responses, but it can't capture what specifically winds you up about your daily experience.

Classroom Connections

1. The Hyperlocal Challenge

Whatever your subject, create assignments that require students to apply concepts to something within a 500-metre radius of where they live.

- Historical impacts on their specific street
- Scientific phenomena in their back garden
- Mathematical patterns in their local shop
- Literary themes in overheard conversations

The more hyperlocal, the more context they'd need to feed AI, making it easier to just do the thinking themselves.

2. The Disagreement Task

Students must find something they genuinely disagree with in the course material and argue against it using their own experience as evidence. Not generic disagreement—personal, specific, grounded disagreement.

- The textbook says X, but when my family tried this...

- The theory suggests Y, but in my sport/hobby/culture, I've noticed...

AI can generate disagreement, but it can't generate *your* disagreement.

3. The Build-Break-Rebuild Cycle

Students create something (an argument, a solution, a design), then must systematically break it themselves, then rebuild it stronger.

- Monday: here's my position.
- Wednesday: here's why I was wrong.
- Friday: here's my stronger position.

The intellectual honesty required to genuinely critique your own work? That's not something you can efficiently outsource.

Layer 3: Transparent Boundaries (That Students Actually Understand)

The third slice is clarity about when and how AI can be used. Not blanket bans, not vague warnings, but specific, reasoned guidance that students can actually follow.

You don't need to come up with the guidance yourself—plenty of folk out there have already done the hard work for you. There are traffic light systems, or Furze et. al's AI Assessment Scale, or any number of other ways that you can set boundaries for when AI use is accepted, and when it isn't.

But here's the crucial bit: you need to explain why each task falls into each category. If you're sticking with a traffic light system, then maybe a vocabulary quiz is red light *because* we're building automatic word recognition, and AI can't do that for your brain. A research project might be yellow *because* AI can help find sources, but you need to evaluate them yourself. Creative writing could be green for idea generation *because* published authors use whatever tools help them; the skill is in selecting and developing ideas, not necessarily generating them from scratch.

When students understand the reasoning, compliance becomes logical rather than obedient. It's the difference between saying, "don't use a calculator" and saying "we're building your mental maths muscles, and a calculator can't do that for you."

The transparency extends to consequences too. Instead of punitive "if you cheat, you fail," it needs to become practical: "if you use AI where it prevents learning, we'll need to find another way for you to develop those skills." It's not about punishment; it's about ensuring the learning actually happens, with or without AI.

Classroom Connection

1. The AI Menu

Create a literal menu for each assignment showing AI options like a restaurant menu.

- Appetisers: *AI brainstorming - free refills!*
- Main course: *AI structure suggestions - must cite your server.*
- Off limits: *Analysis writing - we make this fresh in-house only.*

Make it visual, even funny. It's silly, but it works! Students are more likely to respond better to clever transparency than stern warnings.

2. Student-Generated Guidelines

Have students create their own AI use policies for different types of assignments.

- What would they allow?
- What would defeat the purpose of the task?
- Why have they decided each guideline?

You'll be surprised how strict students can be when they think through the learning implications themselves. Plus, they're more likely to follow rules they helped create.

3. The Citation Experiment

For one week, require students to cite everything... including their own thinking.

- This idea came from class discussion on Tuesday
- This connection occurred to me while walking home
- ChatGPT suggested this structure

- My carer mentioned this example over dinner

Making all intellectual influences visible helps students understand that AI is just one potential source among many, not a hidden shortcut.

Layer 4: Metacognitive Moments (That Make Students Think About Thinking)

The fourth slice is building in regular reflection that makes students aware of their own learning process.

This might be weekly reflections on thinking processes—not what was learned, but how it was learned. What felt easy? What was surprisingly hard? When did confusion turn into clarity? These metacognitive moments are incredibly hard to fake because they're so specific to individual experience. AI can generate generic reflections about learning, but it can't capture the specific moment when something clicked for you personally.

Peer teaching with process focus is another approach. Students explain their work to partners, but the focus isn't on the answer; it's on the journey. "How did you figure that out?" becomes more important than "What did you get?" Try getting AI to fake that thinking process in real-time conversation.

'Confusion journals' can document what confuses students and how they work through it. The value isn't in reaching correct answers but in honestly documenting the struggle. If you use AI to complete work, you don't have genuine confusion to document. Honestly, it might be that writing 'I wasn't confused' becomes an admission that you didn't engage with the material.

Classroom Connection

1. The Stuck Stopwatch

When students work on assignments, they keep a timer running only when they're genuinely stuck. At the end, they submit their 'stuck time' along with what eventually got them unstuck.

Depending on the class, you could celebrate the highest stuck times; the students whowrestled most with the material. Create a leaderboard—*Sarah spent 13 minutes stuck on question 3 before realising she was overcomplicating it...!*—and include yourself on there as well for bonus cred.

2. Think-Aloud Recordings

Students record themselves talking through a problem for 3-5 minutes. No editing, no scripts, just authentic thinking in real-time. The stammers, the "wait, no, that's not right" moments, the sudden realisations—these voice notes capture thinking in action. They're also surprisingly fun to listen to. Hearing someone genuinely figure something out is weirdly compelling.

3. The Learning Autopsy

After any assessment, students perform an 'autopsy' on their learning.

- What died?
- What survived?
- What needs resuscitation?

They identify exactly where their understanding broke down and theorise why. This isn't about correct answers—it's about understanding your own understanding. AI can't tell you where your specific brain got confused.

Layer 5: Genuine Stakes (That Make the Work Matter)

The fifth slice is perhaps the most important: making work matter beyond grades.

When students create something for an authentic audience or genuine purpose, the whole dynamic changes. A website that actual people will read. A presentation to real community members. Videos that younger students will learn from. A campaign about issues that directly affect them.

The stakes don't have to be high in a traditional sense—they just have to be real. No teenager wants to be the one whose explanation confused younger students. No one wants their name on community-facing work that isn't genuinely theirs. When work has authentic purpose, students become naturally protective of their authorship.

This is especially powerful when the work connects to personal experience or passion. Why would you let AI write about your own health condition, your family's immigration story, your neighbourhood's history? The work becomes too personal to outsource.

Classroom Connection

The Teaching Exchange

Partner with another class (younger students, different subject, even different school) where your students become the teachers. They create explanatory materials, answer questions, provide feedback. Nothing makes you own your knowledge like having to teach it. And nobody wants to be the one who confused a bunch of Year 7s with AI-generated nonsense they don't actually understand.

The Public Portfolio

Students maintain one piece of work that will be publicly shared—with parents, on school displays, on a class website, even in a public forum if you can partner with a local library or museum. They choose what goes public and can update it throughout the term. When work has their name on it in public, the relationship to that work fundamentally changes. It becomes about pride, not just grades.

The Expertise Project

Every student becomes the class expert on something specific and personally relevant. They're responsible for helping others understand their area when it connects to course material. You can't be the class expert on your grandmother's immigration story or

> your experience with diabetes or your knowledge of top tier K-pop group Stray Kids if you're letting AI do your thinking for you.

* * *

Even with all these layers, sometimes everything aligns wrong. A stressed student faces a perfect storm of circumstances, and AI misuse slips through. What then?

This is where the Swiss Cheese Model really proves its worth. When something gets through all the layers, it tells us something important about our system. It's diagnostic data, not just rule-breaking.

The response shouldn't be punitive but investigative. What combination of factors led to this? Was it overwhelming deadlines? Missing prerequisite skills? Personal crisis? Misunderstanding of expectations? Each failure is an opportunity to strengthen or adjust our layers.

The nice thing, too, is that you don't need all these layers immediately. Start with what feels manageable. Maybe it's just making thinking more visible in class discussions. Maybe it's redesigning one assignment to require personal connection. Maybe it's having one honest conversation about when AI helps versus hinders. The power isn't in any single layer being perfect. It's in multiple imperfect layers working together, catching different problems, addressing different motivations, removing different temptations.

There's also one more added bonus with the Swiss Cheese model that makes it more powerful than any other anti-cheating system you might have come across. Unlike detection tools that get weaker as AI gets stronger (and, lest we forget, *still don't actually work!*), these layers actually become more relevant as AI advances. The more powerful AI becomes, the more important it is that students value their own thinking, understand their own learning, and connect work to things that matter to them.

Remember the paradox from the previous chapter? The harder we try to catch cheating, the worse everything gets? The Swiss Cheese Model resolves this by changing the game entirely. We're not trying to catch cheating. We're building systems where cheating becomes progressively less attractive, less necessary, and less possible.

Each layer makes thoughtless AI use a bit harder and authentic engagement a bit easier. Stack enough layers, and the path of least resistance becomes... actually doing the thinking. The goal isn't to AI-proof your classroom. It's to create a classroom so engaging, so supportive, so genuinely interested in student thinking that AI becomes what it should be: a tool for enhanced thinking, not a replacement for it.

The Mirror and the Model

16

What Students See

Come on a little thought journey with me. You're a student in a Year 9 English lesson, and the teacher has just finished explaining why you need to think critically about AI-generated content. "Don't just accept what ChatGPT tells you," she says. "Question it. Check it against other sources. Think about bias."

Five minutes later, that same teacher opens her laptop, types *generate a lesson plan that helps students revise macbeth act 2 scene 1, students are low ability but eager to learn* into an AI tool, copies the output directly into her planning document, and moves on to her overflowing stack of marking. No questioning. No checking. No critical evaluation.

How do you feel?

Now, I know that's a terrible example to give you. It's unlikely to take place in the real world.

Unlikely, but not entirely impossible.

The thing is, the students would notice if we used AI like that. They always do. These are the kids who tell us if our mouse cursor is still visible over the YouTube video we play them in lesson. Of *course* they'll notice.

So here's another uncomfortable truth: if we want our students to develop thoughtful, strategic approaches to AI, we need to be thoughtful and strategic about our own AI use first. Our students are watching everything we do with technology, and they're incredibly perceptive about whether we're practicing what we preach.

Right now, many of us aren't.

And you know what, that's completely understandable! AI tools have appeared in our professional lives with remarkable speed, often without anyone giving us adequate training, clear policies, or time to develop best practices. We've had to work it out ourselves. Or, on the other side of the fence, folk give us so *much* information that we end up getting overwhelmed and not knowing what's really the right thing to do. Many educators are using AI reactively rather than strategically, grabbing quick solutions for immediate problems without considering the broader implications for their practice or their students' learning.

And then there's what others are pushing, too; government-built platforms that highlight lesson planning tools as the be all and end all. AI gurus who tell you that all you need to do is build the right GPT and your students will have the world at their feet. Me, writing a book about my own opinions and how they're definitely the right ones...

So it's difficult.

But like I say: our students are always watching. They're forming their understanding of what 'appropriate AI use' looks like based on what they observe us doing, not just what we tell them to do. If we want them to develop the thinking habits we've been discussing throughout this book, we need to model those same habits ourselves.

This section of the book isn't about adding another burden to already overwhelmed educators. It's also not about 'dunking' on you and telling you that you're doing a bad job. It's about recognising that developing our own AI use isn't just beneficial for our professional effectiveness, but essential for our credibility as educators and our students' learning.

* * *

Let's start with a scenario that's probably familiar: You're in a staff meeting where someone mentions that students shouldn't just copy and paste from ChatGPT for their assignments. Heads nod around the room. Everyone agrees that students need to be more thoughtful about AI use.

But then, privately, you wonder: when was the last time you used AI for something work-related? Did you apply the same critical thinking you're asking of your students? Did you verify the information? Consider potential biases? Think about whether AI was the right tool for that particular task?

If you're feeling a bit uncomfortable right now, you're not alone. Honestly, as I wrote this section, I got thinking about my own AI use both in the classroom and in staff training and development sessions. And sometimes, particularly in times when I felt time or personal pressure, I didn't do all the checks I should've done.

It ends up with us experiencing what we might call an 'AI credibility gap'—the distance between what we're asking students to do and what we're actually doing ourselves.

This gap matters because students are remarkably good at detecting authenticity. We all know this already in a complete non-digital type of way! After all, the relationship-building at the heart of education is all about authenticity. In that same way, when we speak about AI from genuine experience—including our mistakes, learning moments, and ongoing questions—students engage differently than when we're reciting principles we haven't actually lived through.

Educational research consistently shows that teacher modelling is one of the most powerful influences on student learning. This is especially true for complex skills like metacognition and critical thinking, where students need to see not just the what but the how and the why of effective thinking. That means that when it comes to AI use, students need to see educators who:

- Struggle with prompts and adjust their approach
- Question AI outputs and seek verification
- Choose AI for some tasks but not others, with clear reasoning
- Acknowledge when AI use hasn't worked well and reflect on why that might be the case
- Demonstrate the thinking processes behind effective AI interactions
- Remember that AI isn't the most important thing here; the human is

Notice that none of this is about being an AI expert or having perfect AI skills. It's about being a visible learner who demonstrates the kind of thoughtful, reflective approach we want students to develop. Same as it always was.

It's important to remember that modelling isn't just about what we show students directly. It's also about what we reveal about our own thinking processes. Every time we use AI in front of students, we're holding up a mirror to our own intellectual habits. Are we curious or lazy? Critical or accepting? Strategic or reactive?

Students notice when we reflexively reach for AI at the first sign of difficulty. They notice when we accept AI outputs without question. They also notice when we take time to think before using AI, when we explain our reasoning, and when we acknowledge the limitations of what AI can provide.

I watch teachers who've developed strong AI metacognition, and there's a different quality to how they interact with these tools. They pause before prompting. They read outputs critically. They explain their decision-making process. They acknowledge uncertainty. These habits make them more effective AI users, but more importantly, they model intellectual integrity for their students.

One teacher I observed was using AI in an IB English lesson to help generate discussion questions for a text analysis. Instead of just reading the AI's suggestions to the class, he thought aloud: "These first three questions are good—they focus on evidence and interpretation. But this fourth one is quite leading—it's pushing toward a particular conclusion rather than encouraging open thinking. I'm going to modify it to be more open-ended."

The students weren't just learning about text analysis in that lesson; they were learning about critical evaluation, intellectual independence, and the importance of thinking for themselves even when working with powerful tools.

* * *

Maybe it helps to think about your use of AI through three lenses. After all, you're quite possibly using it in different ways depending on the role you're playing in that moment.

Personal Level: Your Own AI Use

This is where it starts—developing thoughtful habits around your personal AI interactions. It means applying the same metacognitive processes we've been discussing to your own AI use, whether you're using AI for lesson planning, administrative tasks, professional learning, or any other purpose.

Just as we want students to plan their AI use strategically, we need to be intentional about when, how, and why we turn to AI tools. Just as we want students to monitor their AI interactions for quality and effectiveness, we need to develop our own critical evaluation skills. And just as we want students to evaluate what they've learned from AI, we need to reflect on our own AI experiences.

Professional Level: AI in Your Teaching Practice

At this stage, you're being intentional about when, how, and why you use AI in your teaching. It includes thinking metacognitively about AI's role in your curriculum, assessment practices, and classroom management.

Using AI in a professional context and within your teaching practice requires you to consider not just whether AI helps you as a teacher, but whether your AI use supports or undermines your students' learning. It means being transparent about your AI decision-making when appropriate, and modelling the kind of thoughtful approach you want students to develop.

Leadership Level: AI Culture and Policy

This level isn't only for people in leadership positions. It's for any time you might lead, whether it's acting as a role model for other staff, sharing your thoughts online or at conferences, or even just in discussions with peers.

That said, for those who *are* in leadership positions, this also means thinking strategically about how AI fits into your school's broader educational vision and culture. It involves modelling thoughtful AI use for other staff members and creating conditions that support reflective AI practices across the organisation.

* * *

Developing personal AI awareness doesn't require dramatic changes to your practice or extensive technical training. It starts with bringing the same intellectual habits to your AI use that you're trying to cultivate in your students.

Maybe you start by applying critical thinking to one AI interaction per day. Notice your decision-making process. Reflect on the outcomes. Share your thinking with a colleague or your students when appropriate. Ask yourself the same questions you're teaching students to ask: Is this accurate? Is this helpful? What perspectives might be missing? How does this connect to what I already know?

The habits you develop through this reflective approach will serve you well regardless of how AI technology evolves. More importantly, they'll enable you to guide your students toward the thoughtful, strategic approach to AI that will serve them throughout their lives.

In the next chapter, we'll explore practical strategies, common pitfalls, and concrete examples of what thoughtful AI use looks like in practice. But it all starts with recognising that your own relationship with AI is the foundation for everything else you'll do with these tools in education.

Your students are watching. What do you want them to see?

17

You (Yes You!) And AI

You're sitting at your laptop at 8:47 PM on a Sunday, staring at a blank lesson planning document. Tomorrow's Year 10 Geography class is supposed to cover urban development, and you've got exactly 13 minutes before you promised yourself you'd stop working and actually relax for the evening.

Your cursor hovers over the ChatGPT tab you've got open in your browser. You could type *create a lesson plan for year 10 geography on urban development* and have something workable in 30 seconds. Problem solved, evening saved, Monday morning stress avoided.

But should you?

This moment—one tiny decision that happens amongst the hundreds of others a week for educators—is where everything we've been discussing in this book either comes together or falls apart. If you want your students to develop thoughtful, strategic approaches to AI, you first need to develop those approaches yourself.

This chapter is the culmination of everything we've looked at for redesigning pedagogy, but now it's up to you. What type of mirror are you going to be? And how do you reflect the AI user you want your students to become?

* * *

Planning Your AI Use

Remember Daniel Willingham's three elements of critical thinking: novelty, self-direction, and effectiveness? These apply just as much to your AI use as they do to your students'. Before you type that prompt, pause and ask yourself the same questions you're teaching them to ask.

Novelty: Am I Creating or Just Copying?

When you're tempted to ask AI for 'a lesson plan on photosynthesis,' stop and consider: what kind of thinking are you actually doing here? Are you generating something new that draws on your knowledge of your students, your curriculum context, your previous teaching experiences? Or are you just following the same pattern—problem arises, AI solves problem—that you're warning students against?

The difference is crucial. In the first case, AI is doing the intellectual work that builds teaching expertise. In the second, it's supporting expertise you already possess and are actively applying.

Put it in Practice

Before using AI for lesson planning, spend five minutes writing down key elements of the topic that you know you need to teach and what specific challenges your students typically face with it. Only then craft an AI prompt that incorporates that knowledge. You might ask it to generate additional examples for a concept you know your students struggle with, or to suggest ways to connect photosynthesis to local environmental issues. But the pedagogical reasoning stays with you.

Self-Direction: Am I Choosing or Just Reacting?

How often do you reach for AI tools? If your honest answer is 'whenever I feel stuck' or 'when I'm running out of time,' you might be defaulting rather than deciding.

Self-direction means making conscious choices about when AI adds value versus when struggling through a challenge yourself would actually serve your professional growth better. Sometimes the difficulty is the point.

Put it in Practice

Work through new unit planning yourself first, identifying where you feel genuinely stuck in your ways or where you want to expand beyond your initial ideas. Then use AI strategically for those specific gaps, rather than as a general-purpose lesson plan generator. The result? A much stronger unit that you can teach with genuine enthusiasm and expertise, plus the confidence that comes from doing the intellectual work yourself.

Effectiveness: Will This Actually Help Me Learn?

This might be the most important question, and the one we're most likely to skip when we're stressed or rushed. Not 'will this solve my immediate problem?' but 'will this help me become a better teacher?'

Sometimes the answer is yes. When you use AI to generate multiple examples of a mathematical concept you're already confident teaching, it saves time and gives you variety you might not have thought of on your own. When you ask AI to help you find real-world applications for a scientific principle, it often surfaces connections you can then evaluate and adapt.

But sometimes the answer is no. When you let AI write assessment questions for topics you're still developing your own understanding of, you're not just missing an opportunity to deepen your knowledge, you're potentially assessing students on content you can't confidently explain or defend.

The effectiveness question forces you to think beyond immediate convenience to long-term professional growth. In a nutshell: *Am I using AI in ways that build my teaching capacity, or in ways that prevent me from developing expertise I'll need?*

Put It in Practice

Before using AI for any professional task, ask yourself: *Will doing this with AI help me become better at this type of work, or will it prevent me from developing skills I need?* If you can't articulate how the AI interaction will contribute to your professional growth, consider whether you should tackle the challenge independently first. For tasks where you decide AI is appropriate,

> write down one thing you expect to learn from the interaction that will make you more effective next time.

* * *

Monitoring Your AI Use

Real-time awareness of your AI interactions is where metacognition gets practical. As you're working with AI tools, you need to develop the habit of noticing what's happening in your own thinking.

Cognitive Bypassing Alerts

Here's where things get uncomfortable: How do you know when you're using AI strategically versus when you're letting it do thinking you should be doing yourself?

Or in other words: Are you using AI to enhance your expertise or to avoid doing the work that builds expertise?

This distinction matters because becoming a good teacher doesn't just happen. In fact, studies are starting to come out that show that it's the expert teachers who benefit the most from AI, and the novices (NQTs, PGCE students, and so on) who struggle with being able to learn the key skills outside of AI use. Being a good teacher develops through deliberate practice, reflection, and the kind of productive struggle that builds deep understanding. When AI eliminates that struggle entirely, it can prevent the professional growth that makes you more effective over time.

Consider this when you're tempted to use AI for tasks like analysing student work or identifying learning gaps. These are core teaching skills that require human judgement, contextual knowledge, and the kind of pattern recognition that develops through experience. If you consistently offload this thinking to AI, you're not just saving time—you're potentially stunting your growth as an educator.

The key is being intentional about which cognitive work you preserve for yourself and which you're comfortable sharing with AI. Core pedagogical thinking—understanding your students, designing learning experiences, evaluating progress—probably belongs in the 'preserve' category. Administrative tasks, content research, and format generation might be reasonable candidates for AI support.

Put it in practice

Create two lists: "Preserve for Me" and "OK to Share with AI." In the first column, write down the types of teaching tasks that build your professional expertise—things like analysing why a student is struggling, deciding what concept to teach next, or evaluating whether a lesson achieved its objectives. In the second column, list tasks that support your work but don't require your pedagogical judgement—formatting resources, finding background information, or generating multiple examples of problems you already understand how to create. When you're tempted to use AI, check which list the task belongs to. If it's in the "Preserve" column, do the thinking work yourself first, then consider if AI can help refine your ideas.

Working Memory and Cognitive Load

AI can either reduce helpful cognitive load or harmful cognitive load in your professional learning. When you use AI to handle formatting, research organisation, or administrative tasks, it frees up mental space for the pedagogical thinking that builds expertise. This is strategic offloading.

But when AI handles the core intellectual work—designing assessments, analysing student needs, making curricular decisions—it's removing the very cognitive load that builds teaching expertise. This is cognitive bypassing, and it prevents professional growth.

> **Put it in practice**
>
> Try this simple test: if completing this task yourself would make you better at understanding your students or improving your teaching, preserve that thinking for yourself.

Desirable Difficulties

Sometimes the most valuable thing you can do is resist the urge to ask AI for help. Not because AI is bad, but because the struggle itself is what builds your professional capacity.

When you're designing a challenging assessment, the cognitive work of thinking through what skills you're targeting, how to measure them fairly, and what obstacles students might face—that's professional development happening in real time. If you outsource all of that thinking to AI, you miss the opportunity to strengthen your assessment design skills.

Put it in practice

Always write your first draft of complex pedagogical work yourself, even if it's rough. Then you might ask AI to suggest additional approaches or help you think about accessibility. But you need to do the initial thinking yourself, or you're not really learning how to get better at the task.

Spaced Practice

If you use AI for every instance of a particular type of task, you're essentially doing 'massed practice' with dependency. Instead, try spacing out your AI use so you regularly practise skills independently.

This might mean setting aside certain lesson planning sessions as 'AI-free zones' where you work through challenges using your own knowledge and resources. Or alternating between AI-supported and independent work when creating assessments, designing activities, or analysing student needs.

The goal isn't to make your life harder unnecessarily, but to maintain and develop the professional skills that make you effective even when AI isn't available.

Put it in Practice

Choose one teaching task you currently use AI for regularly—lesson planning, assessment creation, or resource development. For the next month, alternate your approach: use AI for this task one time, then do it independently the next time. During your independent sessions, resist the urge to check your work against AI immediately. Instead, complete the entire task using your own knowledge and judgement first. After you've finished, you can compare your independent work with what AI might suggest, but notice what you accomplished on your own. This pattern helps you maintain your professional skills while still benefiting from AI support when it's genuinely helpful.

Retrieval Practice: Think First, Then Check

Before asking AI for help with professional tasks, spend a few minutes retrieving what you already know. What have you learned from previous experience with this type of challenge? What resources or strategies have worked before? What are the key considerations you need to keep in mind?

This preliminary thinking serves two purposes: it activates your existing expertise so you can engage more critically with AI outputs, and it provides retrieval practice that strengthens your professional knowledge.

Put it into practice

Try your own 'brain dump' before AI interactions. If you're planning a unit on persuasive writing, spend five minutes writing down everything you know about teaching this topic—common student challenges, effective strategies, assessment approaches, etc. Then when you ask AI for additional ideas, you're building on a foundation rather than starting from scratch.

* * *

Evaluating your AI Use

At the end of each week, or after completing a significant project with AI support, take time to reflect honestly on what happened. Not just whether you got your work done, but whether you grew as a professional.

The Transfer Test

When you've used AI to help with something, ask yourself: If I needed to do this task again next week without AI, could I? Do I understand the reasoning behind the choices that were made? Can I adapt this approach to different contexts?

If the answer is no, you might have let AI do too much of the thinking.

Put it into practice

Example: You use AI to help create a rubric for assessing collaborative projects. The AI output is sophisticated and thorough, but when you try to explain the criteria to your students, you stumble. You realise you've accepted the rubric without fully understanding the assessment philosophy behind it.

Solution: Go back and do what you should have done initially: identify the specific collaborative skills you want to assess, research different approaches to evaluation, and then use AI to help

> refine the language and structure. The result is a rubric you can confidently explain, defend, and adapt for future use.

* * *

The Sunday evening lesson planning scenario we started with? Here's how it looks different now: You still have 13 minutes, and you still need that geography lesson. But now you pause and think:

- What do I already know about urban development?
- What did my students struggle with last time we covered related topics?
- What specific aspect of this topic do I need the help with?

Maybe you decide to use AI to generate real-world examples of urban development from different global contexts, since you know your students respond well to diverse case studies. Or maybe you realise that the struggle of working through the lesson yourself will help you better understand where students might get confused.

Either way, you're making a conscious choice based on professional judgement rather than just reaching for the fastest solution. And that choice—multiplied across hundreds of similar moments throughout your teaching career—is what builds the kind of thoughtful AI relationship you want to model for your students.

In a nutshell, here's where we're at: The only way to make sure we're being good AI mirrors for our students is by continuously asking ourselves three key questions:

Have I engaged with the problem enough to understand it myself? If a student asked me to explain why this feedback is helpful, could I do it? If a colleague questioned my assessment design, could I defend it?

Can I explain the "why" behind the choices AI has made? If AI suggested three differentiation strategies and I chose one, do I know why it's the right one for my students? Or did I just pick the first one because it looked reasonable?

Would I be happy for a student to see my process right now? Not just the final product, but the actual steps I took to get there. Would I be proud of how much thinking I contributed versus how much I handed over?

If the answer is yes, you're in safe territory. If the answer is no, you've got your warning sign.

18

A Few Final Words

We've been on a bit of a journey, you and I.

Whether you've read the book from front to back, or jumped hither and thither, here's what I'm hoping you've learned: That the AI revolution isn't actually about AI. It's about thinking. It always was. AI just forced us to finally confront what we've been avoiding for decades, asking ourselves what education is actually for when information is free and answers are instant.

We started with existential dread. We wrestled with the detection trap. We explored the paradox of scaffolding. We got practical about cognitive offloading. And we built the Swiss Cheese Model—those beautiful, imperfect layers that make thinking too valuable to outsource.

But here's what I really want you to take away: This isn't about defending education against AI, or vice versa. It's about using AI to make education finally become what it always claimed to be—a thinking cultivation system, not an information transfer mechanism.

Remember that student who asked, "Why can't I just use ChatGPT?" The answer isn't "because it's cheating." The answer is "you can – but let me show you how to use it to think better, not less." Remember the Stupidly Large Office Building - the SLOB - and the different receptionists found in the brains of Kiki and Janine? Well, it turns out our students can just as easily be a Kiki as a Janine.

The shift we're talking about throughout this book—from prohibition to purposeful integration—changes everything. Suddenly we're not guards protecting academic integrity. We're thinking coaches showing students how to use every tool available to develop their cognitive muscles. We're not trying to catch cheaters; we're trying to create thinkers who wouldn't want to cheat themselves out of the thinking experience.

When we frame it this way, AI becomes what it should be: cognitive scaffolding that helps students reach higher, not a forklift that carries them to the top whilst their intellectual muscles atrophy.

Your Mission (Should You Choose to Accept It)

So here's your call to action. Not tomorrow, not next term, but literally the next time you're with students:

Step 1: Start the Conversation

Be honest about AI. Acknowledge that it exists, that they're probably using it, and that you're more interested in helping them use it well than catching them using it badly. Say something like: "Right, we all know ChatGPT exists. Instead of pretending it doesn't, let's work out how to use it to make our thinking better, not replace it."

Step 2: Model Thinking With AI

�Show them your own process. Pull up your AI tool of choice during a lesson. Give it a prompt. Then—and this is crucial—think out loud about what it produced. "This bit's interesting but needs evidence... This claim seems dodgy... Oh, this gave me an idea about..." Show them that AI output is a starting point for thinking, not an ending point.

Step 3: Create Thinking Partnerships

Teach students to use AI as a thinking partner, not a thinking replacement. Show them how to:

- Use it to explore perspectives they haven't considered
- Challenge their own assumptions by asking it to argue against them
- Generate examples to test their understanding
- Create practice problems to check their learning
- Get unstuck without getting answers

Step 4: Make Metacognition Non-Negotiable

Whatever subject you teach, build in reflection about thinking. Not just what was learned but how it was learned. What did AI help with? What could only their brain do? When did AI make thinking better? When did it get in the way? Make this reflection as important as the work itself.

Step 5: Redesign One Thing

Pick one assignment. Just one. Redesign it using the Swiss Cheese Model. Add layers that make thinking visible and valuable. Create authentic stakes. Build in process checkpoints. Make it hyperlocal or hyperpersonal. Transform it from something students might want to outsource into something they'd want to own.

* * *

Here's the thing that makes me genuinely excited about education's future: The more powerful AI becomes, the more valuable human thinking becomes. Not because AI can't think (although I feel like that debate will rage for decades), but because your thoughts, your connections, your confusions, your breakthrough moments—they're yours. They're what make you you.

The real revolution that's on the horizon honestly isn't in the fancy new technology, however well (or not well) it develops over the years. It's in finally having a reason to do what great educators have always wanted: to stop prioritising information transfer and start prioritising learning how to think about things.

AI didn't create this opportunity. It just made it impossible to ignore.

And here's another thing: your students are already using AI. But they're also waiting. For someone to show them the difference. For permission to be curious about their own thinking. For someone to make visible thinking more valuable than polished products.

They're waiting for you to stop trying to catch them and start trying to coach them.

They don't need you to protect them from AI. They need you to show them how to think with it, through it, about it, and despite it. And, most importantly, they need you to help them fall in love with their own thinking—its uniqueness, its struggles, its breakthrough moments.

So we have a choice. We can spend the next decade playing defence—building better detection tools, creating more elaborate policies, fighting a losing battle against technology that's evolving faster than our rules.

Or we can play offence. We can use AI as the catalyst for the thinking revolution education has needed for decades. We can create classrooms where thinking is visible, valuable, and genuinely exciting. We can raise a generation who see AI as a thinking partner, not a thinking replacement.

The robots aren't coming for education. They're already here. The question is whether we'll use them to make thinking obsolete or to make it more powerful than ever.

I know which future I'm choosing. The one where my students' thinking is too interesting, too valuable, too genuinely *theirs* to ever want to outsource.

What about you?

Bibliography

Anders, B. A. (2018). *The AI Literacy Imperative: Empowering Instructors & Students.*

Armitage, K. L., Bulley, A., & Redshaw, J. (2020). *Developmental origins of cognitive offloading.* Proceedings of the Royal Society B Biological Sciences, 287(1928), 20192927. https://doi.org/10.1098/rspb.2019.2927

Ask the Cognitive Scientist: How Can Educators Teach Critical Thinking? (2023, July 12). American Federation of Teachers. https://www.aft.org/ae/fall2020/willingham

Azevedo, R., Dever, D., Wiedbusch, M., Brosnihan, A., Delgado, T., Marano, C., Patel, M., & Smith, K (2024). *A taxonomy for enhancing metacognitive adaptivity and personalization in serious games using multimodal trace data.* In Lecture notes in computer science (pp. 27–40). https://doi.org/10.1007/978-3-031-74138-8_3

Bathaee, Y. (2018). *The Artificial Intelligence Black Box and the Failure of Intent and Causation.* Harvard Journal of Law & Technology, 31(2), 889. https://www.questia.com/library/journal/1G1-547758123/the-artificial-intelligence-black-box-and-the-failure

Bjork, R. A., & Bjork, E. L. (2020). *Desirable Difficulties in Theory and Practice.* Journal of Applied Research in Memory and Cognition, 9(4), 475–479. https://doi.org/10.1016/j.jarmac.2020.09.003

Brown, P. C., Roediger, H. L., III, & McDaniel, M. A. (2014). *Make It Stick: The Science of Successful Learning.* Harvard University Press.

Bulley, A., McCarthy, T., Gilbert, S. J., Suddendorf, T., & Redshaw, J. (2020). *Children devise and selectively use tools to offload cognition.* Current Biology, 30(17), 3457-3464.e3. https://doi.org/10.1016/j.cub.2020.06.035

Burns, T., & Sinfield, S. (2016). *Essential Study Skills: The Complete Guide to Success at University (4th ed.).* http://ci.nii.ac.jp/ncid/BB05540786

Catrambone, R. (1995). *Aiding subgoal learning: Effects on transfer.* Journal of Educational Psychology, 87(1), 5–17. https://doi.org/10.1037/0022-0663.87.1.5

Chase, W. G., & Simon, H. A. (1973). *Perception in chess. Cognitive Psychology,* 4(1), 55–81. https://doi.org/10.1016/0010-0285(73)90004-2

Churches, A. (2008). *Bloom's Digital Taxonomy.*

Clark, A., & Chalmers, D. (1998). *The extended mind.* Analysis, 58(1), 7–19. https://doi.org/10.1093/analys/58.1.7

Clark, R. E. (1983). *Reconsidering Research on Learning from Media.* Review of Educational Research, 53(4), 445–459. https://doi.org/10.3102/00346543053004445

Common Sense Media. (2022). *The dawn of the AI Era: teens, parents, and the adoption of generative AI at home and school.* https://www.commonsensemedia.org/sites/default/files/research/report/2024-the-dawn-of-the-ai-era_final-release-for-web.pdf

Cope, B., & Kalantzis, M. (2009). *Multiliteracies: new literacies, new learning.* Pedagogies an International Journal, 4(3), 164–195. https://doi.org/10.1080/15544800903076044

Corbin, T., Tai, J., & Flenady, G. (2025). *Understanding the Place and Value of GenAI Feedback: A Recognition-based Framework.* Assessment & Evaluation in Higher Education, 1–14. https://doi.org/10.1080/02602938.2025.2459641

Cowan, N. (2001). *The Magical Number 4 in Short-term Memory: A Reconsideration of Mental Storage Capacity.* Behavioral and Brain Sciences, 24(1), 87–114. https://doi.org/10.1017/s0140525x01003922

Denejkina, A. (2023). *Young people's perception and use of Generative AI.* In YouthInsight Powered by Student Edge. https://youthinsight.com.au/education/young-peoples-perception-and-use-of-generative-ai/

Dunlosky, J., Rawson, K. A., Marsh, E. J., Nathan, M. J., & Willingham, D. T. (2013). *Improving Students' Learning With Effective Learning Techniques.* Psychological Science in the Public Interest, 14(1), 4–58. https://doi.org/10.1177/1529100612453266

Fitzpatrick, D. (2025). *Infinite Education: The Four-Step Strategy for Leading Change in the Age of Artificial Intelligence.* Teachergoals Publishing.

Gerlich, M. (2025). *AI Tools in Society: Impacts on cognitive offloading and the future of critical thinking.* Societies, 15(1), 6. https://doi.org/10.3390/soc15010006

Gonsalves, C. (2024). *Generative AI's impact on Critical Thinking: Revisiting Bloom's taxonomy.* Journal of Marketing Education. https://doi.org/10.1177/02734753241305980

Hirsch, E. D. (2000). *You can always look it up - or can you?* American Educator.

K Agarwal, P. (Ed.). (2025). *Smart Teaching Stronger Learning: Practical Tips From 10 Cognitive Scientists.* Unleash Learning Press.

Karpicke, J. D., & Roediger, H. L. (2008). *The Critical Importance of Retrieval for Learning.* Science, 319(5865), 966–968. https://doi.org/10.1126/science.1152408

Larkin, J., McDermott, J., Simon, D. P., & Simon, H. A. (1980). *Expert and novice performance in solving physics problems.* Science, 208(4450), 1335–1342. https://doi.org/10.1126/science.208.4450.1335

Larson, B. Z., Moser, C., Caza, A., Muehlfeld, K., & Colombo, L. A. (2024a). *Critical Thinking in the Age of Generative AI.* Academy of Management Learning and Education, 23(3), 373–378. https://doi.org/10.5465/amle.2024.0338

Lee, H., Sarkar, A., Tankelevitch, L., Drosos, I., Rintel, S., Banks, R., & Wilson, N. (2025). *The Impact of Generative AI on Critical Thinking: Self-Reported Reductions in Cognitive Effort and Confidence Effects From a Survey of Knowledge Workers* (pp. 1–22). https://doi.org/10.1145/3706598.3713778

Mark, G., Gudith, D., & Klocke, U. (2008). *The Cost of Interrupted Work: More Speed and Stress.* https://ics.uci.edu/~gmark/chi08-mark.pdf

Martin, A. J., Collie, R. J., Kennett, R., Liu, D., Ginns, P., Sudimantara, L. B., Dewi, E. W., & Rüschenpöhler, L. G. (2025). *Integrating generative AI and load reduction instruction to individualize and optimize students' learning.* Learning and Individual Differences, 121, 102723. https://doi.org/10.1016/j.lindif.2025.102723

Metcalfe, J., & Shimamura, A. P. (1994). *Metacognition.* In The MIT Press eBooks. https://doi.org/10.7551/mitpress/4561.001.0001

Mishra, P. (2023, December 19). *Generative AI is WEIRD!* https://punyamishra.com/2023/12/19/generative-ai-is-weird/

Mollick, E. (2024). *Co-Intelligence: Living and Working with AI.* Penguin.

Neugnot-Cerioli, M., & Muss Laurenty. (2024, May). *The Future of Child Development in the AI Era.* Cross-Disciplinary Perspectives Between AI and Child Development Experts. arXiv:2405.19275.

OpenAI. (2025, May 2). *Expanding on what we missed with sycophancy.* https://openai.com/index/expanding-on-sycophancy/

Perkins, M. (2023). *Academic Integrity Considerations of AI Large Language Models in the Post-pandemic Era: ChatGPT and Beyond.* Journal of University Teaching and Learning Practice, 20(2). https://doi.org/10.53761/1.20.02.07

Pierce, W. D., & Bandura, A. (1977). *Social Learning Theory.* The Canadian Journal of Sociology, 2(3), 321. https://doi.org/10.2307/3340496

Pressley, M., Wharton-McDonald, R., Mistretta-Hampston, J., & Echevarria, M. (1998). *Literacy instruction in 10 Fourth-Grade classrooms in upstate New York.* Scientific Studies of Reading, 2(2), 159–194. https://doi.org/10.1207/s1532799xssr0202_4

Quigley, A., Mujis, D., & Stringer, E. (2021). *Metacognition and Self-Regulated Learning: Guidance report.* Education Endowment Foundation. https://educationendowmentfoundation.org.uk/education-evidence/guidance-reports/metacognition

Risko, E. F., & Gilbert, S. J. (2016). *Cognitive offloading.* Trends in Cognitive Sciences, 20(9), 676–688. https://doi.org/10.1016/j.tics.2016.07.002

Risko, E., Kelly, M., Patel, P., & Gaspar, C. (2019). *Offloading memory leaves us vulnerable to memory manipulation.* Cognition, 191, 103954. https://doi.org/10.1016/j.cognition.2019.04.023

Ritchhart, R. (2015). *Creating Cultures of Thinking: The 8 Forces We Must Master to Truly Transform Our Schools.* John Wiley & Sons.

Roe, J., M Jacobs, G., & A Renandya, W. (2023). *A Review of AI-Powered Writing Tools and Their Implications for Academic Integrity in the Language Classroom.* Journal of English and Applied Linguistics, 2(1). https://doi.org/10.59588/2961-3094.1035

Roschelle, J., Lester, J., & Fusco, J. (2020). *AI And the Future of Learning: Expert Panel Report.* https://doi.org/10.51388/20.500.12265/106

Rundle, K., Curtis, G., & Clare, J. (2020). *Why Students Choose Not to Cheat.* In Edward Elgar Publishing eBooks. https://doi.org/10.4337/9781789903775.00014

Stanovich, K. E. (1986). *Matthew Effects in Reading: Some Consequences of Individual Differences in the Acquisition of Literacy.* Reading Research Quarterly, 21(4), 360–407. https://doi.org/10.1598/rrq.21.4.1

Stone, S. M., & Storm, B. C. (2019). *Search fluency as a misleading measure of memory.* Journal of Experimental Psychology Learning Memory and Cognition, 47(1), 53–64. https://doi.org/10.1037/xlm0000806

Sweller, J. (1988). *Cognitive Load During Problem Solving: Effects on Learning.* Cognitive Science, 12(2), 257–285. https://doi.org/10.1207/s15516709cog1202_4

Vigors, A. (2022). *The Thinking Classroom: Supporting Educators to Embed Critical and Creative Thinking.*

Walker, M. P., & Stickgold, R. (2005). *Sleep, Memory, and Plasticity.* Annual Review of Psychology, 57(1), 139–166. https://doi.org/10.1146/annurev.psych.56.091103.070307

Walker, M., Stickgold, R., Alsop, D., Gaab, N., & Schlaug, G. (2005). *Sleep-dependent Motor Memory Plasticity in the Human Brain.* Neuroscience, 133(4), 911–917. https://doi.org/10.1016/j.neuroscience.2005.04.007

Ward, A. F. (2013). *Supernormal: How the internet is changing our memories and our minds.* Psychological Inquiry, 24(4), 341–348. https://doi.org/10.1080/1047840x.2013.850148

Weinstein, Y., Sumeracki, M., & Caviglioli, O. (2018). *Understanding How We Learn: A Visual Guide.* Routledge.

Willingham, D. T. (2008). *Critical Thinking: Why Is It so Hard to Teach?* Arts Education Policy Review, 109(4), 21–32. https://doi.org/10.3200/aepr.109.4.21-32

Willingham, D. T. (2009). *Why Don't Students Like School?: A Cognitive Scientist Answers Questions About How the Mind Works and What It Means for the Classroom.* John Wiley & Sons.

World Economic Forum. (2025). *Future of Jobs Report 2025.* https://reports.weforum.org/docs/WEF_Future_of_Jobs_Report_2025.pdf

About the cover image

Title: Turning Threads of Cognition

Hanna Barakat & Cambridge Diversity Fund

'Turning Threads of Cognition' is a digital collage highlighting the historical overlay of computing, psychology, and biology that underpin artificial intelligence. The vintage illustration of a head (an ode to Rosalind Franklin, a British chemist who discovered the double helix of DNA) is mapped with labeled sections akin to a phrenology chart. The diagram of the neutral network launches the image into the modern day as AI seeks to classify and codify sentiments and personalities based on network science. The phrenology chart highlights the subjectivity embedded in AI's attempts to classify and predict behaviors based on assumed traits. The background of the Turing Machine and the two anonymous hands pulling on strings of the "neural network," are an ode to the women of Newnham College at Cambridge University who made the code-breaking decryption during World War II possible. Taken together, the collage symbolizes the layers of intertwined disciplines, hidden labor, embedded subjectivity, and material underpinnings of today's AI technologies.

www.hbarakat.com
www.race-equality.admin.cam.ac.uk/university-diversity-fund
https://betterimagesofai.org

Acknowledgements

This book exists because of a ridiculous number of people who've shaped my thinking, challenged my assumptions, and occasionally reminded me that writing a book was actually a thing I said I'd do.

First, to David Ingram for being open enough to let me play with AI, for showing me what true leadership looks like (including how to celebrate your wins and own up to your mistakes), and for your constant championing of me throughout my career. Our weekly meetings are sorely missed.

Amy Uffindall, Maisy Rees, and Kelly King for their support in the original 'AI and Creativity' research project, and Daire Maria Ni Uanachain for being my research partner and taking the research further than I ever could. Bonus thanks to the teachers at DCSPX who trialled any of my AI mad ideas; especially to Luyi Feng, Eamonn King, Ben Oliver-Robinson, David Brown, Tima Robertson (and all that time to 'sort your life out' with AI!), Niall Walker, Vicky Walker, Alan Wright, Gemma Stanton, Jen Bethel, Biz Taherabadi, Katie Woeppel, Maddie Barton, Steph Bell, Amber Zhou, and the many more I'm sure I've forgotten!

Kiki Zhu for being such a brilliant partner in all our SE21 spaces. Thank you for teaching me that culture plays just as much a role in learning as language does, and for always being so encouraging.

Alex McMillan, the EdTech Joyce to my EdTech Eliot, for always being there to bounce ideas off, even if the idea is 'what if I wrote a book' and then forgetting about it for months. Thinking Routines are all on you, pal.

To Jane Kennedy and Sarah Blakeman for your incredible critical friendship. I don't know what I did to deserve your support, but this book wouldn't be anything more than a frustrated scribble on an unread blog if it wasn't for your constant encouragement.

The online EdTech community deserves massive thanks, and I don't even know where to begin here. Cora Yang for inspiring me, both as a woman in tech and one in EdTech in particular, and for being so generous with sharing everything online that I couldn't help but follow in her footsteps. Dalton Flanagan, the second half of that EdTech power couple, for everything he shares around AI and for helping me stay up to date. Dr Shannon Doak for his inspiring keynotes and even more inspiring EdTech leadership, and for championing my often waffled thinking. Ryan Krakofsky for your undying support and cheerleading that makes me feel like what I do actually matters. Al Kingsley who inspires me with his many years of dedication to edtech and the betterment of students both in the UK and further afield. Matthew Wemyss, who many years ago said on a Zoom call 'you're doing what I wish I was doing' and made me realise how lucky I was, and how I should definitely try more to make good with what I did. Look at you now!

Elizabeth Ennis and Natasha Dennis for being my EdTech guinea pigs and testing everything I throw at you (including me crying in your offices).

Crispian Farrow for never minding my nagging messages and constant requests for more AI tools to test and play with. Even though we're on opposite sides of the world, that'll never change. I've got you on speed dial.

Jessica Mileo at Inkwell Management, I know this isn't the Infinite Bookshop but I'll get there one day. Thank you for always championing what I write, no matter what it is.

To the Lizard Squad, Alyssa Zaczek and Emily Monaco. No lizard brain here today.

To anyone who has read my work as it goes out on different platforms and given me feedback or shared their thoughts - every time you respond to what I write, you change how I think and help me understand the world more.

To Dad and Chloe for being encouraging no matter what I write, and Emily for that late night chat about AI in industry that got me thinking outside of the education box. To Alex and Flo, who are going to grow up in this world and will hopefully learn how to think well in it.

To Dongdong and Xixi, for leaving cat hair everywhere, interrupting every single Zoom call and podcast recording I ever made, and keeping me company on late night writing missions.

And for Jordan, my best guy and the best thinker out there. Thanks for all the coffee mornings, for putting up with my hyperfixations and long-winded rants, for your design expertise (I'm glad we didn't go with the weird brain wig), and for always having that classic big pog little poggers energy. You're pretty okay.

About the Author

Amelia King is a leader in educational technology and innovation, with nearly a decade of experience transforming learning environments through cutting-edge digital strategies. Amelia has spearheaded award-winning initiatives, including the integration of AI, AR, and VR into classrooms, and maker education.

Her expertise spans AI integration, systems thinking, digital pedagogy, and maker education, and she has both an NPQSL and an MSc in Smart EdTech and Co-Creativity. A sought-after speaker and presenter, Amelia has delivered engaging workshops and keynote addresses at conferences such as ACAMIS and 21st Century Learning, sharing actionable strategies for digital transformation and effective EdTech leadership. With a unique ability to bridge innovation and pedagogy, Amelia inspires audiences to reimagine education in the age of technology.

Find out more at amelia-king.com

Printed in Dunstable, United Kingdom

77734688R00137